Second Workshop on Beyond Vision and LANguage: inTEgrating Real-world kNowledge (LANTERN 2020)

Held online due to COVID-19

Barcelona, Spain
13 December 2020

ISBN: 978-1-7138-2829-7

Printed from e-media with permission by:

Curran Associates, Inc.
57 Morehouse Lane
Red Hook, NY 12571

Some format issues inherent in the e-media version may also appear in this print version.

Printed with permission by Curran Associates, Inc. (2021)

For permission requests, please contact the Association for Computational Linguistics at the address below.

Association for Computational Linguistics
209 N. Eighth Street
Stroudsburg, Pennsylvania 18360

Phone: 1-570-476-8006
Fax: 1-570-476-0860

acl@aclweb.org

Additional copies of this publication are available from:

Curran Associates, Inc.
57 Morehouse Lane
Red Hook, NY 12571 USA
Phone: 845-758-0400
Fax: 845-758-2633
Email: curran@proceedings.com
Web: www.proceedings.com

COLING 2020

Beyond Vision and LANguage: inTEgrating Real-world kNowledge (LANTERN)

Proceedings of the Second Workshop

December 13, 2020
Barcelona, Spain (Online)

Introduction

Welcome to LANTERN 2020, The Second Workshop Beyond Vision and Language: Integrating Real-World Knowledge, co-located with COLING 2020. Building on the success of the first edition co-located with EMNLP-IJCNLP 2019, the second edition aims to bring together and interconnect researchers focusing on language from a multimodal perspective. In particular, the main goal of the workshop is to promote and foster research which uses machine- and deep-learning techniques to interconnect language with vision and other modalities by leveraging some external knowledge. By encouraging contributions exploiting very diverse sources of external knowledge (knowledge graphs, fixed and dynamic environments, cognitive and neuroscience data, etc.), the workshop is open to all research directions which acknowledge the importance of knowledge in acquiring, using, and evaluating language in real-world settings.

In this second edition, we called for both long and short papers. All the accepted contributions are published in these Proceedings. Moreover, we host presentations from papers accepted to appear in the novel "Findings of EMNLP 2020" series. These papers are not published in the LANTERN Proceedings.

LANTERN 2020 received 7 submissions, all of which were double-blindly reviewed by three highly-qualified reviewers. In total, 4 papers (1 long, 3 short) were accepted to appear in the Proceedings of the workshop, with an acceptance rate of around 57% (comparable to that of the first edition, which was around 53%).

Contributions are representative of a broad range of current problems and approaches and include a novel technique to improve text-to-image synthesis by leveraging visual question answering, an approach to learn commonsense from image captions descriptions, an evaluation of the language used by computational models to characterize people in images, a method that leverages eye-tracking information for the task of dependency parsing. Such richness of approaches and perspectives is in line with the purpose of the workshop, and confirms the growing interest for problems going beyond the task-specific integration of language and vision.

The program of the workshop, besides 4 oral presentations and a session where papers published in the "Findings of EMNLP 2020" are presented, includes invited talks by Yonatan Bisk, Gemma Boleda, Angeliki Lazaridou, and Stefan Lee. The workshop received sponsorship by iDeaL SFB 1102. Best paper award is sponsored by HuggingFace.

The LANTERN Workshop Organizers

Organizers:

Aditya Mogadala, Saarland University (Germany)
Sandro Pezzelle, University of Amsterdam (The Netherlands)
Dietrich Klakow, Saarland University (Germany)
Marie-Francine Moens, Katholieke Universiteit Leuven (Belgium)
Zeynep Akata, University of Tübingen (Germany)

Program Committee:

Afra Alishahi, Tilburg University
Alane Suhr, Cornell University
Albert Gatt, University of Malta
Alessandro Suglia, Heriot-Watt University
Anand Mishra, IIT Jodhpur
Ashutosh Modi, IIT Kanpur
Carina Silberer, University of Stuttgart
Claudio Greco, University of Trento
David Schlangen, University of Potsdam
Douwe Kiela, Facebook AI Research
Florian Metze, Carnegie Mellon University
Iacer Calixto, UvA/NYU
Ionut-Teodor Sorodoc, Universitat Pompeu Fabra
Jacob Goldberger, Bar Ilan
Parisa Kordjamshidi, Michigan State University
Ravi Shekhar, Queen Mary University London
Sina Zarrieß, University of Jena
Somak Aditya, Microsoft Research India
Spandana Gella, Amazon AI

Invited Speaker:

Angeliki Lazaridou, DeepMind
Gemma Boleda, Universitat Pompeu Fabra & ICREA
Stefan Lee, Oregon State University
Yonatan Bisk, Carnegie Mellon University

Table of Contents

Conference Program

LANTERN is a virtual event with four oral for the accepted long or short papers and also presentations from "Findings of EMNLP 2020". It also includes four invited presentations. The full schedule is presented below and all times are listed in CET.

14:00 - 14:15 Welcome and Opening Remarks

14:15 - 14:55 Invited Talk: Angeliki Lazaridou (DeepMind)

14:55 - 15:35 Invited Talk: Gemma Boleda (Universitat Pompeu Fabra & ICREA)

15:35 - 16:15 Accepted Papers (pre-recorded + live Q & A)

1. Eyes on the Parse: Using Gaze Features in Syntactic Parsing

2. Leveraging Visual Question Answering to Improve Text-to-Image Synthesis

3. Seeing the world through text: Evaluating image descriptions for commonsense reasoning in machine reading comprehension

4. How do image description systems describe people? A targeted assessment of system competence in the PEOPLE domain

16:15 - 16:40 Coffee Break

16:40 - 17:20 Invited Talk: Yonatan Bisk (Carnegie Mellon University)

17:20 - 18:00 Invited Talk: Stefan Lee (Oregon State University)

18:00 - 18:40 Findings of EMNLP 2020 (live talk + Q & A)

18:40 - 19:00 Best Talk/Poster Award and Concluding Remarks

Eyes on the Parse: Using Gaze Features in Syntactic Parsing

Abhishek Agrawal **Rudolf Rosa**
Charles University, Prague
Faculty of Mathematics and Physics
Institute of Formal and Applied Linguistics
abhi1994.aa@gmail.com, rosa@ufal.mff.cuni.cz

Abstract

In this paper, we explore the potential benefits of leveraging eye-tracking information for dependency parsing on the English part of the Dundee corpus. To achieve this, we cast dependency parsing as a sequence labelling task and then augment the neural model for sequence labelling with eye-tracking features. We also augment a graph-based parser with eye-tracking features and parse the Dundee Corpus to corroborate our findings from the sequence labelling parser. We then experiment with a variety of parser setups ranging from parsing with all features to a delexicalized parser. Our experiments show that for a parser with all features, although the improvements are positive for the LAS score they are not significant whereas our delexicalized parser significantly outperforms the baseline we established. We also analyze the contribution of various eye-tracking features towards the different parser setups and find that eye-tracking features contain information which is complementary in nature, thus implying that augmenting the parser with various gaze features grouped together provides better performance than any individual gaze feature.

1 Introduction

When it comes to natural language processing (NLP), most of the research work that is done is based on textual data that is usually annotated in some way while human language processing data like eye movement recordings, etc. are often overlooked. The solutions for most tasks in NLP these days are based on neural networks which require annotated data on a large scale to learn good representations and provide meaningful results. Annotating such large quantities of data is not an easy task usually requiring a lot of manual labour which is time consuming and can be expensive not to mention resolving the inter-annotator agreement. However, every single day, millions of people read their daily newspapers, books, magazines, articles on the internet, etc. in a multitude of languages. In the past couple of years some studies have shown that using behavioral data for NLP tasks involving syntax and semantics can be useful (Mishra et al., 2016a; Mishra et al., 2016b; Mishra et al., 2016c; Barrett and Søgaard, 2015a; Barrett and Søgaard, 2015b). This leads us to believe that if there was a way to tap into cognitive data generated by unconscious human parsing of text, it could be leveraged in some manner to support NLP tools thereby reducing our dependency on annotated textual data.

Another reason for choosing to work with eye-tracking features is that it is highly likely that eye-tracking technology will be available on a much larger scale in the near future and hence can be leveraged easily for NLP tasks. This is evidenced by the availability of eye-tracking through regular webcams (San Agustin et al., 2009) and smartphones (Krafka et al., 2016). San Agustin et al. (2010) developed the ITU Gaze Tracker which was a low-cost eye-tracking system based on a webcam that is mounted close to the user's eye. The developers of this system soon established their company *"The Eye Tribe"*[1] with a focus on providing low cost eye-tracking and providing eye control technology for mass

[1] https://theeyetribe.com

Proceedings of the Second Workshop on Beyond Vision and LANguage: inTEgrating Real-world kNowledge (LANTERN), pages 1–16
Barcelona, Spain (Online), December 13, 2020

market consumer devices. Although eye-tracking recording might seem an even more expensive solution to manually annotating data, several studies and even efforts made by the industry indicate that costs associated with eye-tracking hardware and software are just going to go down and that next generation mass consumer goods like smartphones, tablets, laptops and gaming consoles will come equipped with eye-tracking capabilities.

Dependency parsing is a fairly well studied phenomenon because of its relevance in several downstream NLP applications and because of the overwhelming success of the *Universal Dependencies* (UD) project (Nivre et al., 2016) which is an endeavor to provide guidelines for consistent dependency annotations across multiple languages. This study primarily presents an investigation in leveraging eye-tracking features for dependency parsing and the knowledge they bring in identifying syntactic categories and relations. There have been only two previous studies, to the best of our knowledge, which try to leverage gaze features[2] for dependency parsing (Strzyz et al., 2019b; Barrett and Søgaard, 2015b). Strzyz et al. (2019b) cast dependency parsing as sequence labelling in a multi-task learning (MTL) setup where the gaze features are predicted as an auxiliary task while considering that the eye-tracking data will be available only during training time. For our study, we try an alternative approach to Strzyz et al. (2019b) wherein we focus on determining the effects of incorporating eye-tracking data directly in the model for dependency parsing and assume that eye-tracking data would also be available to us at inference time as opposed to the approach followed by Strzyz et al. (2019b). To provide further evidence, we also employ a graph-based parser and augment it with gaze features to see if they improve parsing. We try to address the following research questions through our study:

1. Does eye-tracking data from a reader reading a sentence contain syntactically relevant information?

2. Can the accuracy of syntactic parsing be improved by adding eye-tracking features?

2 Background and Related Work

Eye-tracking information has been used over several years to try to understand cognitive processes. Eye movement recordings of a person taken when they are reading a text have been known to reflect a person's comprehension of the text (Gaskell et al., 2012). Intuitively, one can understand how information about the piece of text that is being focused on and how long it takes to read a piece of text would help in understanding how text is comprehended while being read.

2.1 Factors affecting eye-movements while reading

Gaskell et al. (2012) review several works and provide a good overview of the various factors which influence the eye-movements while reading. The two main factors influencing eye-movements are the word length and word frequency with shorter and more frequent words being skipped more often and longer fixation durations for less frequent and longer words (Brysbaert and Vitu, 1998; Rayner and McConkie, 1976; Liversedge et al., 2004; Rayner et al., 2006; Rayner et al., 2003). Other factors affecting eye-movements are familiarity with the word and the age of acquisition of the word. The degree of familiarity of a word to its reader inversely corresponds to the duration of the first fixation by the reader (Chaffin et al., 2001; Juhasz and Rayner, 2003; Williams and Morris, 2004) and words that are acquired early in life by a reader are processed much faster than words they acquire in the later stages of their life (Juhasz and Rayner, 2003; Juhasz, 2005; Juhasz and Rayner, 2006). The ambiguous meanings of a word also affect the eye-movement patterns with the fixation duration depending upon the frequency of the ambiguous meanings as well as the dominant/sub-ordinate meaning of the word (Rayner and Duffy, 1986; Duffy et al., 1988; Rayner and Frazier, 1989; Sereno et al., 2006).

Studies also found that whenever the predictability of a word based on the past context increases, its reading time decreases and some words that are highly predictable from the past context are altogether skipped (Ehrlich and Rayner, 1981; Rayner and Well, 1996). Morris (1994) found that the fixation duration on a word decreases if it is semantically associated with any prior word. Frazier and Rayner (1982) and Meseguer et al. (2002) found that a reader is innately aware of the point in text where their

[2] Gaze features are the same as eye-tracking features and the two terms are used interchangeably throughout this study.

incorrect syntactic analysis of a sentence differs from the correct analysis as the reader's eyes move back to this point after a regression.

2.2 Overview of eye-tracking in NLP

In this sub-section we describe some of the studies in the field of NLP which make use of eye-tracking data. Barrett et al. (2016a) use eye-tracking data to improve a POS tagger and found significant improvements in the results. A very interesting study by Barrett et al. (2016b) found that the correlation between gaze features and POS tags can be transferred across languages and they use English gaze features to improve a French POS tagger. Barrett and Søgaard (2015a) found that eye-tracking information can be used to predict the syntactic categories of words and Barrett and Søgaard (2015b) used gaze features to predict the grammatical function of a word. The study done by Barrett et al. (2018) leveraged eye-tracking information to find out human attention and used it to regularize the attention function used in an RNN and found improvements for a range of NLP tasks like sentiment analysis, abusive language detection, etc.

Bingel et al. (2018) use eye-tracking information to predict reading errors of children that have some reading disability. Metrics for evaluating the quality of machine translation output derived from eye-tracking data were found to be better than the automatic metrics in use (Klerke et al., 2015). The idea that eye-tracking data could be used to evaluate machine translation output seems quite reasonable as bad translations would result in longer fixation durations and more regressions by the reader which can be picked up from the data. Klerke et al. (2016) in their work use gaze data in a multi-task learning setup to improve sentence compression. Søgaard (2016) and Hollenstein et al. (2019) couple fMRI data along with eye-tracking data to evaluate the quality of word embeddings. Hollenstein and Zhang (2019) leveraged eye-tracking data for improving named entity recognition. An important feature of their study was to leverage type-aggregated gaze features to eliminate the need for recording eye-tracking data at test time and also make the features useful for cross-domain settings.

A couple of studies have also experimented with some sort of parsing of text using eye-tracking data. Strzyz et al. (2019b) leverage gaze data by learning eye-movement features as an auxiliary task in a multi-task learning setup where both dependency parsing and gaze prediction are addressed as sequence labelling. Their experiments resulted in small positive improvements to dependency parsing, however they did not measure the statistical significance of their results. Lopopolo et al. (2019) go about dependency parsing the other way around by showing that there is a relation between regressions and the syntactic structure of sentences. They tested if the path of regressions from a word to an earlier word coincide – at least partially – with the edges of dependency relations between these words by using dependency parsing features to predict eye-regressions during training. One of their important findings indicates that eye regressions are involved predominantly in dependency parsing at the local level (vast majority being shorter than three words with a predominance of one position backwards), rather than at long distance. Cheri et al. (2016) utilize the eye-movements of several annotators resolving coreference to improve automatic coreference resolution.

Mathias et al. (2018) rate the quality of a piece of text by using eye-tracking data and Mishra et al. (2017) try to quantify the effort needed in reading a piece of text by measuring the complexity of the scanpath of various readers. A few studies also found that eye-tracking data can be used to improve sentiment analysis as well as sarcasm detection (Mishra et al., 2016a; Mishra et al., 2016b; Mishra et al., 2016c).

3 Parser Descriptions

In this section, we describe the two parsers we use in our work. Our primary parser is a modification of the system created by Strzyz et al. (2019b) who in turn adapted the *NCRF++* system (Yang and Zhang, 2018) which is an open source neural sequence labelling toolkit. Our secondary parser is a more traditional graph-based parser known as the *BIST* parser from Kiperwasser and Goldberg (2016). One of the main differences between our parsers and the parser by Strzyz et al. (2019b) is that we assume the availability of gaze features both at training and test time whereas Strzyz et al. (2019b) only use the gaze features during training. Another difference is that we incorporate gaze features as the input to the parser whereas Strzyz et al. (2019b) predict the gaze features as an auxiliary task in a multi-task learning setup.

The parsers are evaluated with respect to the *Labelled Attachment Score* (LAS) and the *Unlabelled Attachment Score* (UAS). The LAS is concerned with the number of words that are assigned a correct head as well as the correct dependency relation whereas the UAS is just concerned with the words that are assigned a correct head.

3.1 Dependency parsing as sequence labelling

The first step while casting dependency parsing as a sequence labelling problem is to convert the dependency tree representation into a set of labels. Our data is in the form of the CoNLL-X format with additional columns containing the gaze features. To encode a dependency tree as labels for sequence labelling, Strzyz et al. (2019c) found that it is sufficient to just encode a word's head and dependency relation associated with it for all the words in a sentence. So following the strategy by Strzyz et al. (2019c) for relative positional encoding, we provide each word with a label that contains its dependency relation label as well as the relative position of its head. The relative position of the head is an encoding in the form of a tuple (p_i, o_i) of a POS tag p_i and a positive or negative number o_i. If the number is positive then it means the head of the word is the o_ith closest word to its right having the POS tag p_i and if the number is negative then the head of the word is the o_ith closest word to its left having the POS tag p_i. For example, (N, 1) would mean "the first noun on the right" of the word is its head. Figure 1 shows an example of an encoded dependency tree.

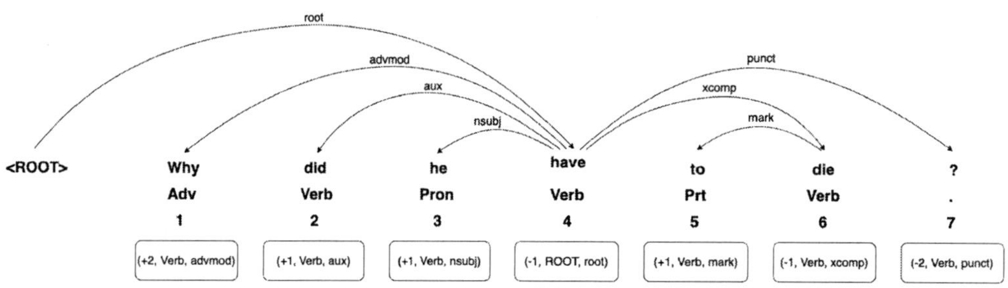

Figure 1: Example of an encoded dependency tree

The generated labels are also conditioned on the chosen multi-task learning setup. In our case, we make use of hard parameter sharing for the multi-task learning setup. As described by Strzyz et al. (2019a), for the combined multi-task learning setup the label will be treated as a single task where its components are separated by the symbol "@". Each component in the label separated by "{}" will be treated as a separate task. The information about the relative position and word's head (e.g. +1@Verb) is combined into one task and the dependency relation is considered as the second task. As per Strzyz et al. (2019a) this gives us the best performance. An example sentence with this setup is as below.

Why	Adv	+2@Verb{}advmod
did	Verb	+1@Verb{}aux
he	Pron	+1@Verb{}nsubj
have	Verb	-1@ROOT{}root
to	Prt	+1@Verb{}mark
die	Verb	-1@Verb{}xcomp
?	.	-2@Verb{}punct

The architecture of the parser is the same as the one employed by Strzyz et al. (2019b) and makes use of bi-directional long short term memory (bi-LSTM) networks (Hochreiter and Schmidhuber, 1997; Schuster and Paliwal, 1997) for the sequence labelling model. For the inputs, we use word, character and POS tag embeddings. The gaze features are also a part of the input, however since they are already real-valued, they are not 'embedded'. One of the changes we make to the parser by Strzyz et al. (2019b) is to concatenate the word,character and POS embeddings with the corresponding gaze features of the word and pass it through a bi-LSTM, which generates vectors that take context into account. For the combined multi-task learning setup, the total loss is computed as the sum of the individual cross-entropy losses:

$$\mathcal{L} = \mathcal{L}_{(o,p)} + \mathcal{L}_d$$

For all our experiments, we evaluate the sequence labelling parser with respect to the UAS and LAS scores excluding punctuations. We exclude the punctuations following the previous work done in this area (Strzyz et al., 2019b). The source code for our sequence labelling parser can be found online[3].

3.2 Graph-based BIST parser

To provide a better perspective about incorporating gaze features with dependency parsing, we also try out a more standard or traditional parser which is commonly known as the *BIST* parser from Kiperwasser and Goldberg (2016). Kiperwasser and Goldberg (2016) employ their approach for both a transition-based parser and a graph-based parser, however we only make use of the graph-based parser in our work. The model that they use for the graph-based parser is the simple first-order arc-factored model (Mcdonald, 2006).

So according to Kiperwasser and Goldberg (2016), if for a sentence s comprising of n words $w_1, \ldots, w_n$ where we also have the corresponding POS tag p_i for each word w_i, we get the embeddings for the words and POS tags denoted by $e(w_i)$ and $e(p_i)$ and then create a sequence of input vectors $x_{1:n}$ where each vector x_i is a concatenation of the word embedding and POS tag embedding and $\circ$ is the concatenation operator:

$$x_i = e(w_i) \circ e(p_i)$$

For our work, we only make one addition to the parser. We use seventeen different gaze features denoted by $g_1, \ldots, g_{17}$ and we concatenate each of these gaze features directly to the word and POS tag embeddings. So our input vector would look like:

$$x_i = e(w_i) \circ e(p_i) \circ g_1 \circ \ldots \circ g_{17}$$

For all our experiments, we evaluate the BIST parser with respect to the UAS and LAS scores. We also include punctuations in the evaluation this time since for our previous parser we excluded them and we hope to demonstrate the overall effect of gaze features on dependency parsing by covering all possible cases. The source code for the graph-based BIST parser can be found online[4].

4 Using gaze features for dependency parsing

In this section, we describe the dataset that we use along with a description of the gaze features that we intend to make use of. We then describe a set of experiments with these gaze features and report the unlabelled and labelled attachment scores (UAS and LAS) on the development and test set and analyze the result of all the scenarios.

4.1 Data

For all our experiments, we make use of the Dundee Corpus (Kennedy et al., 2003). The reason we chose this corpus was because it is the only available eye-tracking corpus having a UD style syntactic annotation layer on top of the English side of the corpus as described by Barrett et al. (2015) in their work on the Dundee Treebank. We only use the English part of the Dundee Corpus for our experiments. We choose 17 different gaze features spread out across four distinct groups (*basic*, *early*, *late* and *contextual* features) similar to Barrett et al. (2016a) and Hollenstein and Zhang (2019).

For all the experiments in this section, we use a 80-10-10 train-dev-test split with a test set of 241 sentences, dev set of 230 sentences and training set of the remaining 1,897 sentences following Barrett et al. (2016a).

[3]`https://github.com/balthamel/dep2label-up`
[4]`https://github.com/balthamel/bist-parser`

Basic	
n fixations	total number of fixations on a word w
fixation probability	the probability that a word w will be fixated
mean fixation duration	mean of all fixation durations for a word w
total fixation duration	sum of all fixation durations for a word w
Early	
first fixation duration	duration of the first fixation on a word w
first pass duration	sum of all fixation durations when it is first visited
Late	
n re-fixations	number of times a word w is fixated (after the first fixation)
re-read probability	the probability of revisiting word w after making a first pass
Context	
total regression-from duration	combined duration of the regressions that began at word w
w-2 fixation probability	fixation probability of the word before the previous word
w-1 fixation probability	fixation probability of the previous word
w+1 fixation probability	fixation probability of the next word
w+2 fixation probability	fixation probability of the word after the next word
w-2 fixation duration	fixation duration of the word before the previous word
w-1 fixation duration	fixation duration of the previous word
w+1 fixation duration	fixation duration of the next word
w+2 fixation duration	fixation duration of the word after the next word

Table 1: Gaze features spread over four groups as adapted from Hollenstein and Zhang (2019).

Table 1 provides a description of all the gaze features used in our experiments. In our experiments, for the gaze features, we normalize all the values across the data. For normalizing the values, we use `scikit-learn`'s normalization from its pre-processing library with all the three norms i.e. '`l1`', '`l2`' and '`max`' norm. The choice of the norm seems to have a considerable effect on the results as is shown in the next couple of sections.

Using just the raw gaze feature values doesn't work well as we found out with one of our initial experiments. It degraded the performance of the parser severely compared to the baseline. Since the ranges for the different gaze features are considerably different, normalizing them makes a lot of sense.

We have two variations in terms of the gaze features that we use. In the first case, we use all seventeen normalized gaze features and these features were picked keeping in mind the previous works in this area (Hollenstein and Zhang, 2019; Strzyz et al., 2019b).

In the second case, we consider a mixture of normalized and raw gaze feature values. We consider raw values only for those features which deal with the number of fixations or probabilities namely: *n fixations*, *fixation probability*, *n re-fixations*, *re-read probability*, *w-2 fixation probability*, *w-1 fixation probability*, *w+2 fixation probability* and *w-2 fixation probability*. For the other features listed in Table 1, we consider their normalized values.

4.2 Experiments

We run our experiments with data that is averaged over all ten readers of the English part of the Dundee corpus. We evaluate several models on the development set varying two hyper-parameters – subset of gaze features to use, and the normalization applied to their values – and identify the best setup for each experiment based on UAS and LAS performance on development data and then run those setups on the test set to verify whether the improvements are consistent. In particular, we carry out three experiments:

- Experiment 1: The first thing we do is to run both parsers with all the available features at hand

Gaze Features		Sequence Labelling Parser lexicalized dev set UAS	LAS	delexicalized dev set UAS	LAS	Graph-Based Parser lexicalized dev set UAS	LAS	delexicalized dev set UAS	LAS
	baseline	83.18	76.45	72.83	64.36	83.41	77.57	73.83	66.49
L1 norm	17 feats. normalized	**84.42**	**77.38**	73.10	64.88	83.52	77.68	73.41	66.90
	17 feats. normalized + raw	83.28	76.78	73.77	65.55	**84.04**	**78.68**	**75.10**	**69.28**
L2 norm	17 feats. normalized	84.30	**77.38**	73.15	64.90	82.62	77.24	73.06	66.81
	17 feats. normalized + raw	83.45	76.82	73.91	**65.73**	83.54	78.16	74.22	67.99
max norm	17 feats. normalized	83.39	76.66	73.94	65.19	83.38	77.66	74.68	68.34
	17 feats. normalized + raw	83.76	77.15	**74.02**	65.71	83.23	77.85	74.22	68.50

Table 2: UAS and LAS scores for lexicalized and delexicalized parsers.

Parser setup	Sequence Labelling Parser lexicalized test set UAS	LAS	delexicalized test set UAS	LAS	Graph-Based Parser lexicalized test set UAS	LAS	delexicalized test set UAS	LAS
baseline	82.19	75.82	72.86	64.89	**82.29**	76.16	74.14	66.80
best setup	**82.46**	**75.93**	****74.11**	***65.84**	81.90	**76.31**	**74.89**	****68.69**

Table 3: Evaluation of best parser setups on test set with UAS and LAS scores (best results in bold; *, ** indicates significant improvement over the baseline; * $p < 0.05$, ** $p < 0.01$ McNemar's test).

i.e. word features, character features (in case of sequence labelling parser), POS tags and the gaze features.[5] The baseline system is a model where no gaze features were used.

- Experiment 2: The next setup that we try out is delexicalized parsing of the data. Delexicalized parsing has been found quite useful in low resource and cross-lingual settings (Zeman and Resnik, 2008; Aufrant et al., 2016). A part of the motivation behind choosing this setup was also that in case of successful delexicalized parsing, it would be interesting to explore if gaze and syntax co-relations can be transferred across a pair of languages, helping to create a cross-lingual dependency parser. That being said, our interest in this setup is merely to explore if eye-tracking features are useful in any form of parsing. In this case we omit the word and character level features and only use the POS tag embeddings and the gaze features. The baseline system is a model where no gaze features were used.

- Experiment 3: Based on the best setups from the first two experiments, to estimate how much individual gaze features and grouped gaze features as per their category (i.e. basic, early, late and context) contribute towards lexicalized and delexicalized parsing, we compare scores from the baseline model where no gaze features are used to models with individual gaze features or grouped gaze features only for the sequence labelling parser.

5 Results

Table 2 shows the results for Experiment 1 and 2. For the lexicalized sequence labelling parser, the best results are obtained by using all 17 features with the L1 norm. There is an improvement of +1.24 for UAS and +0.93 for LAS score as compared to the baseline scores. For the delexicalized sequence labelling

[5]From here on out we call this the 'lexical' parser.

	Gaze features	lexicalized dev set UAS	lexicalized dev set LAS	delexicalized dev set UAS	delexicalized dev set LAS	(Strzyz et al., 2019b) dev set UAS	(Strzyz et al., 2019b) dev set LAS
	baseline	83.18	76.45	72.83	64.36	85.36	79.40
Basic	*n* fixations	+0.60	+0.31	+0.34	+0.23	-0.04	-0.11
	fixation probability	+0.87	+0.46	+0.09	-0.02	-0.04	+0.17
	mean fixation duration	+0.62	+0.19	-0.04	-0.04	-0.15	-0.02
	total fixation duration	+0.68	+0.08	-0.06	-0.14	-0.02	-0.05
	basic features	+0.91	+0.50	**+0.71**	**+0.42**	0.00	+0.17
Early	first fixation duration	+0.97	**+0.73**	-0.12	-0.37	-0.06	+0.06
	first pass duration	+0.83	+0.56	-0.02	+0.04	+0.14	+0.09
	early features	+0.77	+0.62	+0.25	0.00	**+0.25**	+0.17
Late	*n* re-fixations	+0.60	+0.19	+0.32	+0.15	+0.16	-0.15
	re-read probability	+0.25	+0.35	+0.07	+0.08	-0.02	+0.17
	late features	+0.85	+0.70	+0.11	-0.08	+0.18	+0.24
Context	total regression from duration	+0.27	+0.23	+0.19	-0.14	—	—
	w-2 fixation probability	+0.50	+0.33	-0.12	-0.39	—	—
	w-1 fixation probability	+0.60	+0.08	+0.13	-0.52	-0.19	+0.07
	w+1 fixation probability	+0.48	-0.06	-0.16	-0.10	0.00	-0.33
	w+2 fixation probability	+0.50	+0.33	-0.12	-0.39	—	—
	w-2 fixation duration	+0.87	+0.14	+0.30	-0.10	—	—
	w-1 fixation duration	+0.39	+0.23	-0.18	-0.29	+0.07	+0.28
	w+1 fixation duration	+0.77	+0.50	+0.03	-0.29	+0.03	+0.13
	w+2 fixation duration	+0.18	+0.14	+0.34	+0.25	—	—
	context features	**+0.99**	**+0.73**	+0.48	+0.04	**+0.25**	**+0.32**

Table 4: Impact of various gaze features on lexicalized (17 feats. L1 norm) and delexicalized sequence labelling parser (17 feats. max norm + raw). The values in the last two columns are taken directly from Strzyz et al. (2019b) and is an instance of lexicalized parsing. The values reflect improvement or deterioration over the corresponding baseline scores.

parser, the best improvement for the LAS score is +1.37 with the mixture of raw and normalized features with the L2 norm and the best improvement for the UAS score is +1.19 with the mixture of raw and normalized features with max norm. Curiously enough, for the graph-based lexicalized parser, although the best results are also obtained via the L1 normalization of the gaze features, it is the mixture of raw and normalized gaze features that results in the highest scores. We see an improvement of +0.63 for UAS and +1.11 for LAS score as compared to the baseline scores. For the graph-based delexicalized parser, the best improvement we get is of +1.27 for the UAS score and +2.79 for the LAS score by using the L1 norm and a mixture of raw and normalized gaze features. Although the highest scores across both delexicalized parsers vary amongst all three norms used, the one commonality that can be observed from the results is that using a mixture of raw and normalized gaze features provides the best results when it comes to delexicalized parsing. We also observe that the improvements for both parser setups vary considerably depending on the normalization and the features used.

Table 4 shows the results for Experiment 3. For the lexical sequence labelling parser, as seen in Table 2, the L1 norm with all 17 features performs the best in terms of both UAS and LAS scores and for delexicalized parsing we consider the setup with mixture of normalized and raw 17 features with max norm as the best since even though it has lesser LAS score compared to the best one (65.73) the difference is quite marginal. Although the results of our parser cannot be directly compared with the the results of Strzyz et al. (2019b) since we use different training, dev and test splits we still include their results in Table 4. We see that Strzyz et al. (2019b) achieve higher baseline results and our only estimate for this is that they managed to get the CRF layer working properly for them boosting their result. We do, however, note that our improvements with gaze features are higher than that of Strzyz et al. (2019b) and this could be because we directly incorporate the gaze features instead of predicting them as an auxiliary task.

The results from the dev set for the lexical sequence labelling parser show that the grouped *context* gaze features provide the best improvements as compared to the baseline with an improvement of +0.99 for UAS score and +0.73 for the LAS score. Individually, *first fixation duration* provides almost the same improvements as the grouped *context* features with an improvement of +0.97 for UAS score and +0.73 for LAS score. These results are in line with the results of Strzyz et al. (2019b), who found improvements with the *early* and *context* grouped gaze features.

Interestingly, the results from the dev set show that in case of delexicalized parsing, the set of *basic* gaze features, grouped together provide the best improvements as compared to the baseline. They provide an improvement of +0.71 for the UAS score and +0.42 for the LAS score. Individually, the *w+2 fixation duration* and *n fixations* features seem to provide the best improvements over the baseline.

Table 3 shows the results of the baseline parsers and the lexical parsers with the best setups from Table 2 on the test data. For the lexical sequence labelling parser, the best setup uses all 17 gaze features with the L1 norm and for the lexical graph-based parser, using a mixture of all 17 normalized and raw gaze features with L1 norm is the best setup. Table 3 shows that for the lexical sequence labelling parser, although there is an improvement of +0.27 for the UAS score and +0.11 for the LAS score, these improvements are quite small and not statistically significant. We also see that for the lexical graph-based parser, the performance actually deteriorates by -0.39 for the UAS score as compared to the baseline and for the LAS score we see an improvement of +0.15 as compared to the baseline although this improvement is also statistically insignificant. On comparison with their corresponding scores on the development set, these improvements aren't as large and the performance even deteriorates for the graph-based parser in terms of the UAS score leading us to believe that although the gaze features do help marginally in parsing at least for improving the LAS score, the improvement that we saw with the development data was more due to the data and not because of the gaze features.

Table 3 also shows the results of the baseline delexicalized parsers and the delexicalized parsers with the best setups from Table 2 on the test data. For the delexicalized sequence labelling parser, the best setup uses a mixture of all 17 normalized and raw gaze features with max norm and for the delexicalized graph-based parser, using a mixture of all 17 normalized and raw gaze features with L1 norm is the best setup. The results in Table 3 seem to indicate that eye-tracking features most definitely help in delexicalized parsing. There is an improvement of +1.25 over the baseline for the UAS score and an improvement of +0.95 over the baseline for the LAS score, both of which are statistically significant for the delexicalized sequence labelling parser. As for the delexicalized graph-based parser, there is an improvement of +0.75 for the UAS score and +1.89 for the LAS score over the baseline with the improvement for LAS score being statistically significant. The delexicalized sequence labelling parser seems to give better scores for UAS whereas the delexicalized graph-based parser seems to improve the LAS scores more.

A further analysis of the output[6] of the delexicalized sequence labelling parser shows that the dependency relations towards whose identification the gaze features help the most are *root*, *cop* and *aux*. The relative improvements in the prediction of these relations are 9%, 13% and 15% respectively. The POS tags for which gaze features help in correctly identifying the head and dependency relation the most are *NOUN*s, *CONJ* and *VERB*s. The high relative improvements for *root*, *aux*, *cop* and *VERB* makes us conclude that gaze features contain some important syntactic information related to verbs allowing the parser to parse the verbs much better. As verbs are heads of syntactic clauses, it may also be that gaze features help the parser distinguish the main clause (headed by a verb with the 'root' label) from

[6]Detailed results are available in the appendix.

subordinate clauses. The improvement for *CONJ* is also high meaning gaze features somehow help the parser in understanding co-ordination structures.

An alternate hypothesis to explain the improvements in delexicalized parsing could also be that since our data makes use of Google universal POS tags (Petrov et al., 2012), which is more coarse than the UD tagset, the gaze features may simply be distinguishing the POS categories into more fine grained ones like distinguishing between full verbs and auxiliary verbs or co-ordinating and sub-ordinating conjunctions which then in turn helps the parser. It might be the case that were the UD POS tagset had been used in the data, the improvements in the delexicalized parser might have been smaller.

6 Conclusion

In this paper, we explored the benefits of using eye-tracking features for dependency parsing. We performed a set of experiments wherein we tried different parser settings and different eye-tracking feature selection along with various feature normalization techniques to try to answer the question of relevance of gaze features for syntactic parsing.

Our experiments show that although eye-tracking features seem to help in dependency parsing where all features (word level, character level and POS tags) are used for the LAS score, the improvements over the baseline are not statistically significant. However, when we use eye-tracking features for delexicalized parsing, our experimental results show that there is statistically significant improvement over the baseline for both the UAS and LAS scores. For this particular setup, our results seem to indicate that using a mixture of raw and normalized eye-tracking features seems to provide the best improvements.

The results also seem to indicate that grouped gaze features perform better than individual gaze features and that only on combining different gaze feature groups can we obtain significant improvements over the baseline if any. This seems to suggest that the various eye-tracking features contain information which is complementary in nature.

Our experiments also seem to show that gaze features contain syntactic information allowing the parser to parse verbs better and also to better understand co-ordination structures.

Acknowledgements

We would like to especially thank Maria Barrett for providing us with the extracted gaze features without which this work would not have been possible. We also thank the reviewers for their informative comments.

References

Lauriane Aufrant, Guillaume Wisniewski, and François Yvon. 2016. Zero-resource dependency parsing: Boosting delexicalized cross-lingual transfer with linguistic knowledge. In *Proceedings of COLING 2016, the 26th International Conference on Computational Linguistics: Technical Papers*, pages 119–130, Osaka, Japan, December. The COLING 2016 Organizing Committee.

Maria Barrett and Anders Søgaard. 2015a. Reading behavior predicts syntactic categories. In *Proceedings of the Nineteenth Conference on Computational Natural Language Learning*, pages 345–349, Beijing, China, July. Association for Computational Linguistics.

Maria Barrett and Anders Søgaard. 2015b. Using reading behavior to predict grammatical functions. In *Proceedings of the Sixth Workshop on Cognitive Aspects of Computational Language Learning*, pages 1–5, Lisbon, Portugal, September. Association for Computational Linguistics.

Maria Jung Barrett, Zeljko Agic, and Anders Søgaard. 2015. The dundee treebank. In *Proceedings of the Fourteenth International Workshop on Treebanks and Linguistic Theories*, pages 242–248. Association for Computational Linguistics.

Maria Barrett, Joachim Bingel, Frank Keller, and Anders Søgaard. 2016a. Weakly supervised part-of-speech tagging using eye-tracking data. In *Proceedings of the 54th Annual Meeting of the Association for Computational Linguistics (Volume 2: Short Papers)*, pages 579–584, Berlin, Germany, August. Association for Computational Linguistics.

Maria Barrett, Frank Keller, and Anders Søgaard. 2016b. Cross-lingual transfer of correlations between parts of speech and gaze features. In *Proceedings of COLING 2016, the 26th International Conference on Computational Linguistics: Technical Papers*, pages 1330–1339, Osaka, Japan, December. The COLING 2016 Organizing Committee.

Maria Barrett, Joachim Bingel, Nora Hollenstein, Marek Rei, and Anders Søgaard. 2018. Sequence classification with human attention. In *Proceedings of the 22nd Conference on Computational Natural Language Learning*, pages 302–312, Brussels, Belgium, October. Association for Computational Linguistics.

Joachim Bingel, Maria Barrett, and Sigrid Klerke. 2018. Predicting misreadings from gaze in children with reading difficulties. In *Proceedings of the Thirteenth Workshop on Innovative Use of NLP for Building Educational Applications*, pages 24–34, New Orleans, Louisiana, June. Association for Computational Linguistics.

Marc Brysbaert and Françoise Vitu, 1998. *Word skipping: Implications for theories of eye movement control in reading.*, pages 125–147. Eye guidance in reading and scene perception. Elsevier Science Ltd, Oxford, England.

Roger Chaffin, Robin Morris, and Rachel Seely. 2001. Learning new word meanings from context: A study of eye movements. *Journal of experimental psychology. Learning, memory, and cognition*, 27:225–35, 02.

Joe Cheri, Abhijit Mishra, and Pushpak Bhattacharyya. 2016. Leveraging annotators' gaze behaviour for coreference resolution. In *Proceedings of the 7th Workshop on Cognitive Aspects of Computational Language Learning*, pages 22–26, Berlin, August. Association for Computational Linguistics.

Susan A Duffy, Robin K Morris, and Keith Rayner. 1988. Lexical ambiguity and fixation times in reading. *Journal of Memory and Language*, 27(4):429 – 446.

Susan F. Ehrlich and Keith Rayner. 1981. Contextual effects on word perception and eye movements during reading. *Journal of Verbal Learning and Verbal Behavior*, 20(6):641 – 655.

Lyn Frazier and Keith Rayner. 1982. Making and correcting errors during sentence comprehension: Eye movements in the analysis of structurally ambiguous sentences. *Cognitive Psychology*, 14(2):178 – 210.

M. Gareth Gaskell, Adrian Staub, and Keith Rayner. 2012. Eye movements and on-line comprehension processes, 09.

Sepp Hochreiter and Jürgen Schmidhuber. 1997. Long short-term memory. *Neural Comput.*, 9(8):1735–1780, November.

Nora Hollenstein and Ce Zhang. 2019. Entity recognition at first sight: Improving NER with eye movement information. In *Proceedings of the 2019 Conference of the North American Chapter of the Association for Computational Linguistics: Human Language Technologies, Volume 1 (Long and Short Papers)*, pages 1–10, Minneapolis, Minnesota, June. Association for Computational Linguistics.

Nora Hollenstein, Antonio de la Torre, Nicolas Langer, and Ce Zhang. 2019. CogniVal: A framework for cognitive word embedding evaluation. In *Proceedings of the 23rd Conference on Computational Natural Language Learning (CoNLL)*, pages 538–549, Hong Kong, China, November. Association for Computational Linguistics.

Barbara J. Juhasz and Keith Rayner. 2003. Investigating the effects of a set of intercorrelated variables on eye fixation durations in reading. *Journal of experimental psychology. Learning, memory, and cognition*, 29 6:1312–8.

Barbara Juhasz and Keith Rayner. 2006. The role of age of acquisition and word frequency in reading: Evidence from eye fixation durations. *Visual Cognition - VIS COGN*, 13:846–863, 05.

Barbara J. Juhasz. 2005. Age-of-acquisition effects in word and picture identification. *Psychological Bulletin*, 131(5):684–712.

Alan Kennedy, Robin Hill, and Jöel Pynte. 2003. The dundee corpus. In *Proceedings of the European Conference on Eye Movements (ECEM)*.

Eliyahu Kiperwasser and Yoav Goldberg. 2016. Simple and accurate dependency parsing using bidirectional LSTM feature representations. *Transactions of the Association for Computational Linguistics*, 4:313–327.

Sigrid Klerke, Sheila Castilho, Maria Barrett, and Anders Søgaard. 2015. Reading metrics for estimating task efficiency with MT output. In *Proceedings of the Sixth Workshop on Cognitive Aspects of Computational Language Learning*, pages 6–13, Lisbon, Portugal, September. Association for Computational Linguistics.

Sigrid Klerke, Yoav Goldberg, and Anders Søgaard. 2016. Improving sentence compression by learning to predict gaze. In *Proceedings of the 2016 Conference of the North American Chapter of the Association for Computational Linguistics: Human Language Technologies*, pages 1528–1533, San Diego, California, June. Association for Computational Linguistics.

K. Krafka, A. Khosla, P. Kellnhofer, H. Kannan, S. Bhandarkar, W. Matusik, and A. Torralba. 2016. Eye tracking for everyone. In *2016 IEEE Conference on Computer Vision and Pattern Recognition (CVPR)*, pages 2176–2184.

Simon P. Liversedge, Keith Rayner, Sarah J. White, Dorine Vergilino-Perez, John M. Findlay, and Robert W. Kentridge. 2004. Eye movements when reading disappearing text: is there a gap effect in reading? *Vision Research*, 44(10):1013 – 1024.

Alessandro Lopopolo, Stefan L. Frank, Antal van den Bosch, and Roel Willems. 2019. Dependency parsing with your eyes: Dependency structure predicts eye regressions during reading. In *Proceedings of the Workshop on Cognitive Modeling and Computational Linguistics*, pages 77–85, Minneapolis, Minnesota, June. Association for Computational Linguistics.

Sandeep Mathias, Diptesh Kanojia, Kevin Patel, Samarth Agrawal, Abhijit Mishra, and Pushpak Bhattacharyya. 2018. Eyes are the windows to the soul: Predicting the rating of text quality using gaze behaviour. In *Proceedings of the 56th Annual Meeting of the Association for Computational Linguistics (Volume 1: Long Papers)*, pages 2352–2362, Melbourne, Australia, July. Association for Computational Linguistics.

Ryan Mcdonald. 2006. *Discriminative Learning and Spanning Tree Algorithms for Dependency Parsing*. Ph.D. thesis, USA. AAI3225503.

Enrique Meseguer, Manuel Carreiras, and Charles Clifton. 2002. Overt reanalysis strategies and eye movements during the reading of mild garden path sentences. *Memory & cognition*, 30:551–61, 07.

Abhijit Mishra, Diptesh Kanojia, and Pushpak Bhattacharyya. 2016a. Predicting readers' sarcasm understandability by modeling gaze behavior. In *Proceedings of the Thirtieth AAAI Conference on Artificial Intelligence*, AAAI'16, page 3747–3753. AAAI Press.

Abhijit Mishra, Diptesh Kanojia, Seema Nagar, Kuntal Dey, and Pushpak Bhattacharyya. 2016b. Harnessing cognitive features for sarcasm detection. In *Proceedings of the 54th Annual Meeting of the Association for Computational Linguistics (Volume 1: Long Papers)*, pages 1095–1104, Berlin, Germany, August. Association for Computational Linguistics.

Abhijit Mishra, Diptesh Kanojia, Seema Nagar, Kuntal Dey, and Pushpak Bhattacharyya. 2016c. Leveraging cognitive features for sentiment analysis. In *Proceedings of The 20th SIGNLL Conference on Computational Natural Language Learning*, pages 156–166, Berlin, Germany, August. Association for Computational Linguistics.

Abhijit Mishra, Diptesh Kanojia, Seema Nagar, Kuntal Dey, and Pushpak Bhattacharyya. 2017. Scanpath complexity: Modeling reading effort using gaze information. In *AAAI Conference on Artificial Intelligence*.

Robin K. Morris. 1994. Lexical and message-level sentence context effects on fixation times in reading. *Journal of Experimental Psychology: Learning, Memory, and Cognition*, 20(1):92–103.

Joakim Nivre, Marie-Catherine de Marneffe, Filip Ginter, Yoav Goldberg, Jan Hajič, Christopher D. Manning, Ryan McDonald, Slav Petrov, Sampo Pyysalo, Natalia Silveira, Reut Tsarfaty, and Daniel Zeman. 2016. Universal dependencies v1: A multilingual treebank collection. In *Proceedings of the Tenth International Conference on Language Resources and Evaluation (LREC'16)*, pages 1659–1666, Portorož, Slovenia, May. European Language Resources Association (ELRA).

Slav Petrov, Dipanjan Das, and Ryan McDonald. 2012. A universal part-of-speech tagset. In *Proceedings of the Eighth International Conference on Language Resources and Evaluation (LREC'12)*, pages 2089–2096, Istanbul, Turkey, May. European Language Resources Association (ELRA).

Keith Rayner and Susan A. Duffy. 1986. Lexical complexity and fixation times in reading: Effects of word frequency, verb complexity, and lexical ambiguity. *Memory & Cognition*, 14(3):191–201.

Keith Rayner and Louise Frazier. 1989. Selection mechanisms in reading lexically ambiguous words. *Journal of experimental psychology. Learning, memory, and cognition*, 15 5:779–90.

Keith Rayner and George W. McConkie. 1976. What guides a reader's eye movements? *Vision Research*, 16(8):829–837.

Keith Rayner and Arnold D. Well. 1996. Effects of contextual constraint on eye movements in reading: A further examination. *Psychonomic Bulletin & Review*, 3(4):504–509, Dec.

Keith Rayner, Simon P. Liversedge, Sarah Jane White, and Dorine Vergilino-Perez. 2003. Reading disappearing text. *Psychological Science*, 14:385 – 388.

Keith Rayner, Simon P. Liversedge, and Sarah J. White. 2006. Eye movements when reading disappearing text: The importance of the word to the right of fixation. *Vision Research*, 46(3):310 – 323.

Javier San Agustin, Henrik Skovsgaard, John Paulin Hansen, and Dan Witzner Hansen. 2009. Low-cost gaze interaction: Ready to deliver the promises. In *CHI '09 Extended Abstracts on Human Factors in Computing Systems*, CHI EA '09, page 4453–4458, New York, NY, USA. Association for Computing Machinery.

Javier San Agustin, Henrik Skovsgaard, Emilie Mollenbach, Maria Barret, Martin Tall, Dan Witzner Hansen, and John Paulin Hansen. 2010. Evaluation of a low-cost open-source gaze tracker. In *Proceedings of the 2010 Symposium on Eye-Tracking Research & Applications*, ETRA '10, page 77–80, New York, NY, USA. Association for Computing Machinery.

M. Schuster and K.K. Paliwal. 1997. Bidirectional recurrent neural networks. *Trans. Sig. Proc.*, 45(11):2673–2681, November.

Sara Sereno, Patrick O'Donnell, and Keith Rayner. 2006. Eye movements and lexical ambiguity resolution: Investigating the subordinate-bias effect. *Journal of experimental psychology. Human perception and performance*, 32:335–50, 05.

Anders Søgaard. 2016. Evaluating word embeddings with fMRI and eye-tracking. In *Proceedings of the 1st Workshop on Evaluating Vector-Space Representations for NLP*, pages 116–121, Berlin, Germany, August. Association for Computational Linguistics.

Michalina Strzyz, David Vilares, and Carlos Gómez-Rodríguez. 2019a. Sequence labeling parsing by learning across representations. In *Proceedings of the 57th Annual Meeting of the Association for Computational Linguistics*, pages 5350–5357, Florence, Italy, July. Association for Computational Linguistics.

Michalina Strzyz, David Vilares, and Carlos Gómez-Rodríguez. 2019b. Towards making a dependency parser see. In *Proceedings of the 2019 Conference on Empirical Methods in Natural Language Processing and the 9th International Joint Conference on Natural Language Processing (EMNLP-IJCNLP)*, pages 1500–1506, Hong Kong, China, November. Association for Computational Linguistics.

Michalina Strzyz, David Vilares, and Carlos Gómez-Rodríguez. 2019c. Viable dependency parsing as sequence labeling. In *Proceedings of the 2019 Conference of the North American Chapter of the Association for Computational Linguistics: Human Language Technologies, Volume 1 (Long and Short Papers)*, pages 717–723, Minneapolis, Minnesota, June. Association for Computational Linguistics.

Rihana S. Williams and Robin K. Morris. 2004. Eye movements, word familiarity, and vocabulary acquisition. *European Journal of Cognitive Psychology*, 16(1-2):312–339.

Jie Yang and Yue Zhang. 2018. Ncrf++: An open-source neural sequence labeling toolkit. In *Proceedings of the 56th Annual Meeting of the Association for Computational Linguistics*.

Daniel Zeman and Philip Resnik. 2008. Cross-language parser adaptation between related languages. In *Proceedings of the IJCNLP-08 Workshop on NLP for Less Privileged Languages*.

A Analysis of results for delexicalized sequence labelling parser

Table 5 shows the most common correctly predicted dependency relations by our delexicalized sequence labelling parser compared to baseline on the test set. The counts are simply the number of times the delexicalized parser correctly identified that particular dependency relation compared to the baseline parser and the relative frequency is the count divided by the total number of occurrences of that dependency relation in the gold test data. Similarly, Table 6 shows the most common POS tags with correctly predicted heads and dependency relations by our delexicalized parser compared to baseline on the test set.

Deprel	Counts	Relative frequency
root	23	9%
nmod	23	3%
aux	21	15%
nsubj	15	4%
conj	13	6%
case	13	2%
cop	12	13%
det	11	2%
dobj	10	4%
mark	9	3%

Table 5: Most common correctly predicted deprels by our delexicalized sequence labelling parser compared to baseline

POS tag	Counts	Relative frequency
NOUN	112	8%
VERB	82	9%
CONJ	27	15%
ADV	21	6%
ADP	19	3%
DET	17	3%
PRON	16	5%
ADJ	15	3%
PRT	14	6%
NUM	3	4%

Table 6: Most common POS tags with correctly predicted heads and deprels by our delexicalized sequence labelling parser compared to baseline

Parameter	Value
Word embedding dim.	100
POS embedding dim.	25
Optimizer	SGD
Epochs	150
Batch size	8
LSTM hidden state dim.	800
LSTM layers	2
Learning rate	0.02
Learning rate decay	0.05
Momentum	0.9
Dropout	0.5
Char. embedding dim.	30
Char. LSTM dim.	50
Char dropout	0.5

Table 7: Hyperparameters for the sequence labelling parser

B Hyperparameters

Table 7 describes the hyperparameters for the sequence labelling parser. We keep most of the original parameters from the original architecture as the goal of this study is more of an exploratory nature as opposed to achieving state-of-the-art results in dependency parsing. We trained each model upto 150 epochs and kept the model with the highest score on the development set. During multitask learning, for the combined setup we weigh both the tasks as 1.0 since both are equally important and are our main tasks.

Table 8 describes the hyperparameters for the graph-based BIST parser. Again we keep most of the original parameters from the original architecture and only changed the dimension of the LSTM hidden state to 800 because the original parameter was giving poorer results. We trained each model upto 50 epochs and saved the model after every epoch.

Parameter	Value
Word embedding dim.	100
POS embedding dim.	25
Optimizer	Adam
Epochs	50
LSTM hidden state dim.	800
LSTM layers	2
Learning rate	0.1
MLP hidden state dim.	100

Table 8: Hyperparameters for the BIST graph-based parser

C Architecture

Figure 2 depicts the broad architecture of our sequence labelling parser in combined MTL setup.

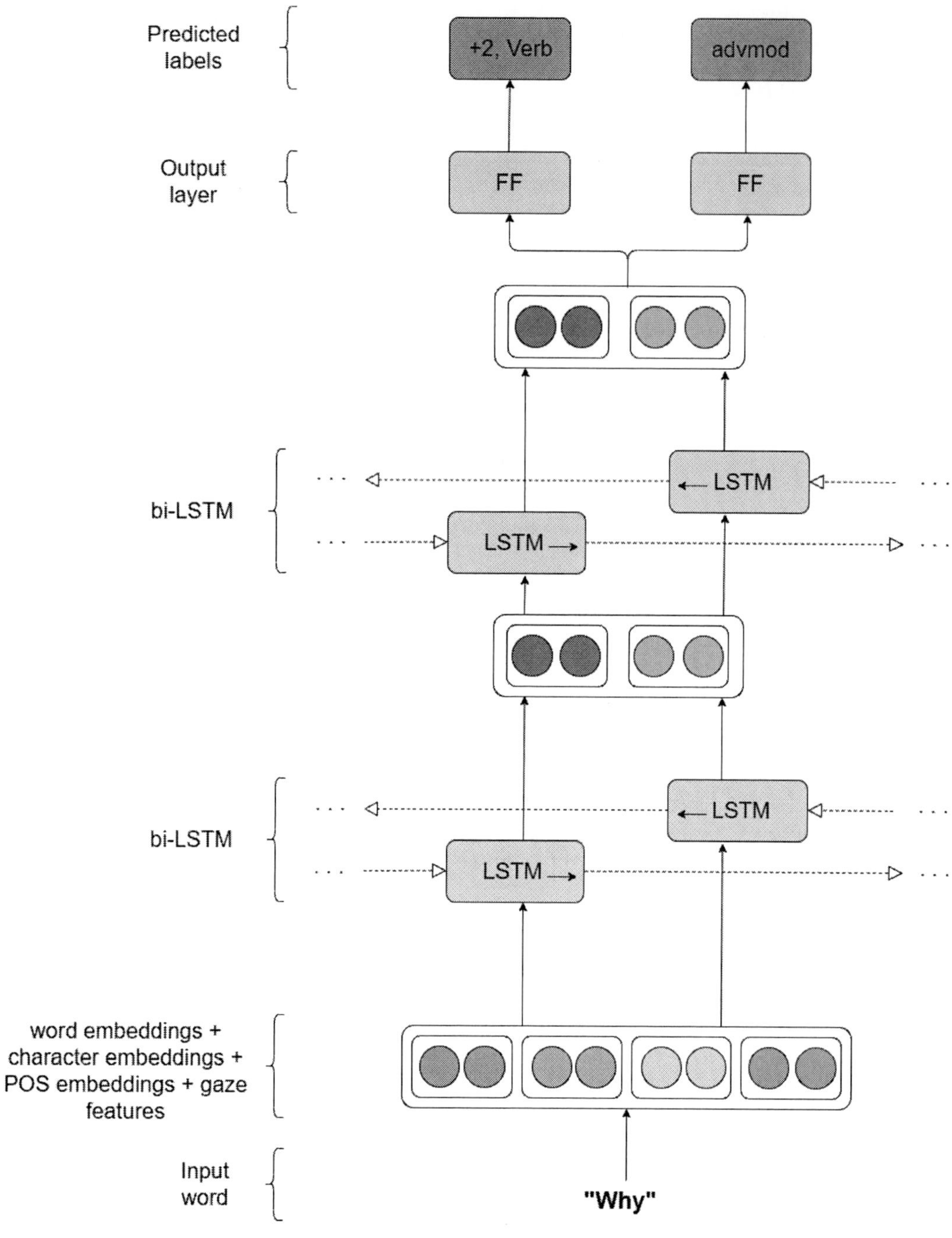

Figure 2: Architecture of sequence labelling parser in combined MTL setup

Leveraging Visual Question Answering to Improve Text-to-Image Synthesis

Stanislav Frolov [1,2], Shailza Jolly [1,2], Jörn Hees [2], Andreas Dengel [1,2]
[1] Technical University of Kaiserslautern, Germany
[2] German Research Center for Artificial Intelligence (DFKI), Germany
firstname.lastname@dfki.de

Abstract

Generating images from textual descriptions has recently attracted a lot of interest. While current models can generate photo-realistic images of individual objects such as birds and human faces, synthesising images with multiple objects is still very difficult. In this paper, we propose an effective way to combine Text-to-Image (T2I) synthesis with Visual Question Answering (VQA) to improve the image quality and image-text alignment of generated images by leveraging the VQA 2.0 dataset. We create additional training samples by concatenating question and answer (QA) pairs and employ a standard VQA model to provide the T2I model with an auxiliary learning signal. We encourage images generated from QA pairs to look realistic and additionally minimize an external VQA loss. Our method lowers the FID from 27.84 to 25.38 and increases the R-prec. from 83.82% to 84.79% when compared to the baseline, which indicates that T2I synthesis can successfully be improved using a standard VQA model.

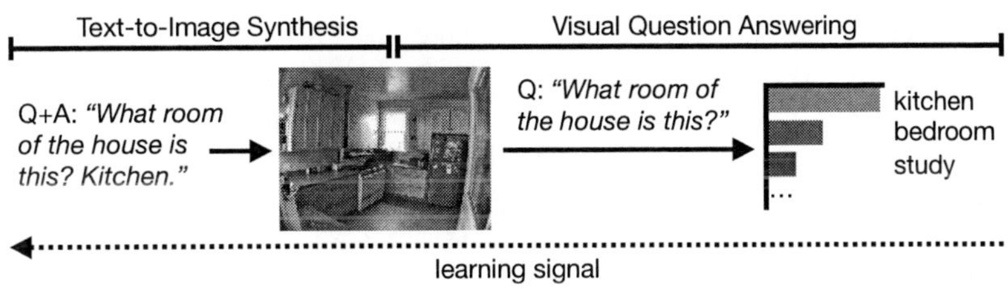

Figure 1: We use concatenated question answer (QA) pairs from VQA data as additional input samples for T2I training. A standard VQA model can then be used to provide an additional loss to the T2I model.

1 Introduction

Text-to-image synthesis (T2I), the task to generate realistic images given textual descriptions, received a lot of attention in recent years (Reed et al., 2016; Zhang et al., 2016; Zhang et al., 2017; Xu et al., 2017; Zhu et al., 2019; Li et al., 2019). T2I synthesis can be seen as the inverse of image captioning. Given a caption, the model is trained to produce realistic images that correctly reflect the meaning of the input captions. Many existing T2I methods use Generative Adversarial Networks (GANs) (Goodfellow et al., 2014). GANs consist of two artificial neural networks that play a game in which a discriminator is trained to distinguish between real and generated images, while a generator is trained to produce images to fool the discriminator. They have successfully been applied to many image synthesis applications such as image-to-image translation (Isola et al., 2016; Zhu et al., 2017), image super-resolution (Ledig et al., 2016), and image in-painting (Yeh et al., 2016).

Similarly, Visual Question Answering (VQA) (Antol et al., 2015) emerged as an important task to build systems that better understand the relationship between vision and language by learning to answer

Proceedings of the Second Workshop on Beyond Vision and LANguage: inTEgrating Real-world kNowledge (LANTERN), pages 17–22
Barcelona, Spain (Online), December 13, 2020

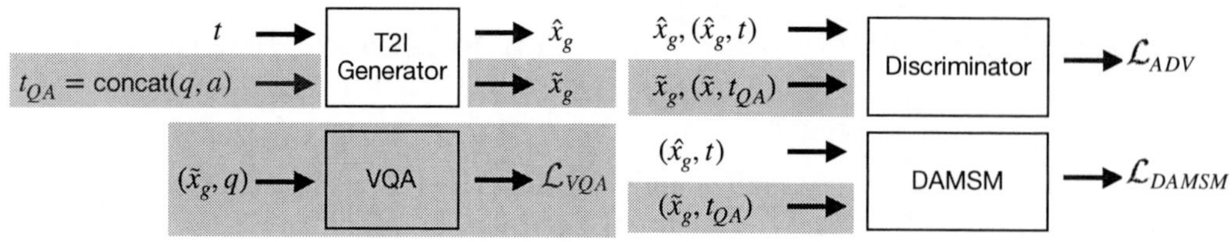

Figure 2: An overview of our architecture with our VQA extension highlighted in red. Given text inputs t (captions) and t_{QA} (concatenated QA pairs) we generate images $\hat{x}_g$ and $\tilde{x}_g$. As in AttnGAN, we use the discriminator and DAMSM model to differentiate between real (omitted in the figure for brevity) and generated images as well as image-text pairs, leading to loss $\mathcal{L}_{\text{ADV}}$, and DAMSM loss $\mathcal{L}_{\text{DAMSM}}$ for improved image-text alignment. Images generated from QA pairs are passed through a VQA model resulting in the additional loss $\mathcal{L}_{\text{VQA}}$.

questions about an image. It can be seen as image conditioned question answering, which encourages the model to both look at the image and understand the question to predict the correct answer.

A good T2I model should produce images that look realistic and correctly reflect the semantic meaning of the input description. Considering the complexity of natural language descriptions and difficulty to produce photographic images, current models struggle to achieve these goals. In this paper we propose a simple, yet effective way to combine T2I with VQA to improve both the image quality and image-text alignment of generated images of a T2I model by leveraging the questions and answers (QA) provided in the VQA 2.0 dataset (Antol et al., 2015). Both captions and QA pairs can describe the overall image or very specific details. In fact, many QA pairs can be rephrased as captions and vice versa which further motivates to leverage VQA for T2I. Additionally, the VQA 2.0 dataset contains complementary images with different answers for the same question which requires the T2I model to learn to pay close attention to the input in order to generate an image that correctly reflects the meaning of the input text. To leverage the VQA 2.0 dataset for T2I, we concatenate QA pairs and use them as additional training samples in our T2I pipeline. Images generated from QA pairs can subsequently be used as inputs to a VQA model which can provide an additional learning signal to the T2I generator. See Figure 1 for an overview of our approach.

2 Related Work

Initial T2I approaches (Reed et al., 2016; Dash et al., 2017) adopted the conditional GAN (cGAN) (Mirza and Osindero, 2014) and AC-GAN (Odena et al., 2016) ideas to replace the conditioning variable by a text embedding which allows to condition the generator on a textual description. Analog to many current approaches, our approach is also based on AttnGAN (Xu et al., 2017), which incorporates an attention mechanism on word features to allow the network to synthesize fine-grained details.

In terms of using VQA for T2I, to our knowledge the only other approach is VQA-GAN (Niu et al., 2020). However, in contrast to their approach, our architecture is simpler, we do not use layout information, work on individual QA pairs, and produce higher resolution images (256x256 vs. 128x128).

3 Approach

We extend the AttnGAN (Xu et al., 2017) architecture to leverage question and answer (QA) pairs from the VQA 2.0 (Goyal et al., 2017) dataset by appending a VQA model (Kazemi and Elqursh, 2017). In addition to generating images from image descriptions, our model is also trained to produce images given a QA pair and minimize an external VQA loss. See Figure 2 for an overview. After revisiting the individual components, we explain our extension in more detail.

3.1 T2I: AttnGAN

AttnGAN (Xu et al., 2017) consists of a multi-stage refinement pipeline that employs attention-driven generators for fine-grained T2I synthesis. A pre-trained bidirectional LSTM (BiLSTM) (Schuster and

Paliwal, 1997) is used to extract global sentence as well as individual word features. Discriminators jointly approximate the conditional and unconditional distributions simultaneously. Additionally, they use an image-text matching loss at the word level called Deep Attentional Multimodal Similarity Model (DAMSM) is employed to guide the image generation process. The attention-driven generator together with the DAMSM loss help the generator to be able to focus on individual words to synthesize fine-grained details and improve the semantic alignment between input description and final image.

3.2 VQA Model

We use a very basic and widely used VQA model, proposed in (Kazemi and Elqursh, 2017) [1]. Given an image I and question q, the model uses image features extracted from a pre-trained ResNet (He et al., 2016), an LSTM (Hochreiter and Schmidhuber, 1997) based question embedding, and employs stacked attention (Yang et al., 2016) to produce probabilities over a fixed set of answers. The VQA loss, given in Equation 1, is simply an average over the negative log-likelihoods over all the correct answers $a_1, a_2, ..., a_K$.

$$\mathcal{L}_{\text{VQA}} = \frac{1}{K}\sum_{k=1}^{K} -\log P(a_k|I,q) \tag{1}$$

3.3 T2I + VQA

We extend AttnGAN (Xu et al., 2017) by appending the VQA model (Kazemi and Elqursh, 2017), and create additional training samples by concatenating question and answer (QA) pairs. Given captions t and QA pairs t_{QA}, we generate fake images $\hat{x}_g$, and $\tilde{x}_g$. Real images are denoted as x_r. Next, the VQA model takes the image generated from the QA pair and corresponding question to produce an answer. Similar to (Niu et al., 2020), we use the VQA loss to predict the correct answer to guide the image generator. At the same time, the discriminators encourage the generated images to be realistic and matching to their corresponding text input. The DAMSM loss (Xu et al., 2017) further helps to focus on the individual words to generate fine-grained details. The final objective of our generator is defined in Equation 2, where $\mathcal{L}_{\text{ADV}}$ is the adversarial (conditional and unconditional) loss, and $\mathcal{L}_{\text{DAMSM}}$ is the DAMSM loss, both as described in (Xu et al., 2017). The adversarial loss and DAMSM loss are applied to both captions and QA pairs and their correspondingly generated images. The VQA loss $\mathcal{L}_{\text{VQA}}$ is applied only to images generated from QA pairs.

$$\begin{aligned}\mathcal{L}_G &= \mathcal{L}_{\text{ADV}} + \mathcal{L}_{\text{DAMSM}}(\hat{x}_g, t) + \mathcal{L}_{\text{DAMSM}}(\tilde{x}_g, t_{\text{QA}}) + \mathcal{L}_{\text{VQA}}(\tilde{x}_g, q)\\ \mathcal{L}_{\text{ADV}} &= \underbrace{-\mathbb{E}[\log D(\hat{x}_g)] - \mathbb{E}[\log D(\tilde{x}_g)]}_{\text{unconditional loss}} \underbrace{-\mathbb{E}[\log D(\hat{x}_g, t)] - \mathbb{E}[\log D(\tilde{x}_g, t_{\text{QA}})]}_{\text{conditional loss}}\end{aligned} \tag{2}$$

The discriminators are trained to classify between real and fake images, as well as image-caption and image-QA pairs to simultaneously approximate the conditional and unconditional distributions by minimizing the modified loss defined in Equation 3.

$$\begin{aligned}\mathcal{L}_D = &\underbrace{-\mathbb{E}[\log D(x_r)] - \mathbb{E}[\log(1 - D(\hat{x}_g))] - \mathbb{E}[\log(1 - D(\tilde{x}_g))]}_{\text{unconditional loss}}\\ &\underbrace{-\mathbb{E}[\log D(x_r, t)] - \mathbb{E}[\log(1 - D(\hat{x}_g, t))] - \mathbb{E}[\log(1 - D(\tilde{x}_g, t_{\text{QA}}))]}_{\text{conditional loss}}\end{aligned} \tag{3}$$

4 Experiments

We train three different variants of our extension. The first two are naive extensions in which we do not change the discriminator loss of AttnGAN. Instead, we simply append the VQA model, sample a QA

[1] `https://github.com/Cyanogenoid/pytorch-vqa`

pair during training and add the external VQA loss to the overall generator loss function. We experiment with an end-to-end training approach where we start with a randomly initialized VQA model, and a pre-trained VQA model. Next, we train a model in which we change the discriminator and generator loss functions. In other words, given a QA pair, the model is not only trained to minimize the VQA loss for that particular QA pair, but also to produce realistic and matched images as judged by the discriminator and DAMSM loss. For fair comparison we re-train and re-evaluate AttnGAN using the codebase provided by the authors[2].

4.1 Datasets and Evaluation

We use the commonly used COCO (Lin et al., 2014) and VQA 2.0 (Goyal et al., 2017) datasets to train our model. COCO depicts complex scenes and multiple interacting objects and contains around 80k images for training and 40k images for testing. Each image has five captions. VQA 2.0 is a large dataset of question answer pairs based on the COCO images with roughly 400k QAs for training and 200k for testing, hence extensively used by VQA researchers (Tan and Bansal, 2019; Kim et al., 2018; Lu et al., 2019). It contains complementary images for the same question, such that the model learns to look closely at the image before answering instead of deploying language biases (Antol et al., 2015).

We evaluate the quality and diversity of generated images using the Inception Score (IS) (Salimans et al., 2016) and Fréchet Inception Distance (FID) (Heusel et al., 2017). To compute the IS[3] and FID[4] we generate 30k images from 30k randomly sampled test captions. R-prec. (Xu et al., 2017) is used to evaluate the semantic alignment between generated images and input captions. Although R-prec. might be unreliable, as current models seem to achieve higher scores than real images (Hinz et al., 2019), we include it for reference since it is still commonly used. Similar to (Niu et al., 2020), we evaluate the VQA accuracy of our models by generating images from test QA pairs and passing them to the pre-trained VQA model with the corresponding question and answer.

4.2 Results

Method	IS ↑	FID ↓	R-prec. ↑	VQA Acc. ↑
Real Images	34.88	6.09	68.58	60.00
AttnGAN (Xu et al., 2017)	**26.66**	27.84	83.82	43.00
AttnGAN + end-to-end VQA	25.22	30.68	82.68	42.85
AttnGAN + pre-trained VQA	26.02	28.72	84.25	42.83
AttnGAN + pre-trained VQA + adapted loss	26.64	**25.38**	**84.79**	**43.75**

Table 1: Results on the COCO test dataset. First row contains scores for real images (excluding VQA Acc.) as reported in (Hinz et al., 2019). We re-train and re-evaluate the baseline AttnGAN (second row). Third and fourth row are our naive extensions in which we simply append a VQA model for an external VQA loss for images generated from QA pairs. In the last row, we change the discriminator and generator losses to also encourage images generated from QA pairs to look realistic and match the input (similar to standard AttnGAN losses for images generated from captions). We train each model for 120 epochs, select the checkpoint with the best IS and report corresponding FID, R-prec., and VQA accuracy.

As can be seen in Table 1, merely adding the external VQA loss to the generator impairs the performance, regardless of using a pre-trained VQA model or training it as part of the pipeline in an end-to-end way. We hypothesize this is due to the images produced from QA pairs not being encouraged to look realistic during training and the generator struggling to minimize the external VQA loss for images generated from QA pairs, on the one hand, and standard AttnGAN losses for images generated from captions, on the other hand.

[2]https://github.com/taoxugit/AttnGAN

[3]https://github.com/sbarratt/inception-score-pytorch

[4]https://github.com/mseitzer/pytorch-fid

Therefore, in our third experiment (last row) we change the overall objective and encourage all generated images to be realistic and matched to the input description using the conditional and unconditional losses from the discriminator and DAMSM loss (as in standard AttnGAN). While achieving almost identical IS, our model greatly improves the FID from 27.84 to 25.38, which indicates better image quality and diversity. Additionally, the images produced by our extension are better aligned to the input descriptions as indicated by the improvement of R-prec. from 83.82 to 84.79, and VQA accuracy from 43.00 to 43.75. Since the VQA 2.0 dataset contains complementary image and QA pairs, the slight variation in linguistic inputs might hence help the model to generate better images. Our results show that it is possible to improve T2I synthesis by simply appending a standard pre-trained VQA model, leveraging the VQA 2.0 dataset as additional supervision and encouraging the model to also produce realistic images from QA pairs. Although we show that already a simple VQA model can help to improve the final T2I performance, we hypothesize that using a state-of-the-art VQA model might further improve the results.

5 Conclusion

In this paper we proposed a simple method to leverage VQA data for T2I via a combination of AttnGAN, a well-known T2I model, and a standard VQA model. By concatenating quesion answer (QA) pairs from the VQA 2.0 dataset we created additional training samples. Images generated from the QA pairs are passed to the VQA model which provides an additional learning signal to the generator. Our results show a substantial improvement over the baseline in terms of FID, but requires additional supervision. Possible future research directions could be to investigate whether our extension also boosts other T2I models, and the influence of more training data and the external VQA loss separately.

Acknowledgements

This work was supported by the BMBF project DeFuseNN (Grant 01IW17002) and the TU Kaiserslautern PhD program.

References

Stanislaw Antol, Aishwarya Agrawal, Jiasen Lu, Margaret Mitchell, Dhruv Batra, C Lawrence Zitnick, and Devi Parikh. 2015. Vqa: Visual question answering. In *ICCV*.

Ayushman Dash, John Cristian Borges Gamboa, Sheraz Ahmed, Marcus Liwicki, and Muhammad Zeshan Afzal. 2017. Tac-gan - text conditioned auxiliary classifier generative adversarial network. *ArXiv*, abs/1703.06412.

Ian J. Goodfellow, Jean Pouget-Abadie, M. Mirza, Bing Xu, David Warde-Farley, Sherjil Ozair, Aaron C. Courville, and Yoshua Bengio. 2014. Generative adversarial nets. In *NIPS*.

Yash Goyal, Tejas Khot, Douglas Summers-Stay, Dhruv Batra, and Devi Parikh. 2017. Making the V in VQA matter: Elevating the role of image understanding in Visual Question Answering. In *CVPR*.

Kaiming He, X. Zhang, Shaoqing Ren, and Jian Sun. 2016. Deep residual learning for image recognition. In *CVPR*.

Martin Heusel, Hubert Ramsauer, Thomas Unterthiner, Bernhard Nessler, and Sepp Hochreiter. 2017. Gans trained by a two time-scale update rule converge to a local nash equilibrium. In *NIPS*.

Tobias Hinz, Stefan Heinrich, and Stefan Wermter. 2019. Semantic object accuracy for generative text-to-image synthesis. *ArXiv*, abs/1910.13321.

S. Hochreiter and J. Schmidhuber. 1997. Long short-term memory. *Neural Computation*, 9:1735–1780.

Phillip Isola, Jun-Yan Zhu, Tinghui Zhou, and Alexei A. Efros. 2016. Image-to-image translation with conditional adversarial networks. In *CVPR*.

Vahid Kazemi and Ali Elqursh. 2017. Show, ask, attend, and answer: A strong baseline for visual question answering. *ArXiv*, abs/1704.03162.

Jin-Hwa Kim, Jaehyun Jun, and Byoung-Tak Zhang. 2018. Bilinear attention networks. In *NeurIPS*.

Christian Ledig, Lucas Theis, Ferenc Huszár, José Antonio Caballero, Andrew Aitken, Alykhan Tejani, Johannes Totz, Zehan Wang, and Wenzhe Shi. 2016. Photo-realistic single image super-resolution using a generative adversarial network. In *CVPR*.

Wenbo Li, Pengchuan Zhang, Lei Zhang, Qiuyuan Huang, Xiaodong He, Siwei Lyu, and Jianfeng Gao. 2019. Object-driven text-to-image synthesis via adversarial training. In *CVPR*.

Tsung-Yi Lin, Michael Maire, Serge Belongie, James Hays, Pietro Perona, Deva Ramanan, Piotr Dollár, and C. Lawrence Zitnick. 2014. Microsoft coco: Common objects in context. In *ECCV*.

Jiasen Lu, Dhruv Batra, Devi Parikh, and Stefan Lee. 2019. Vilbert: Pretraining task-agnostic visiolinguistic representations for vision-and-language tasks. In *NeurIPS*.

Mehdi Mirza and Simon Osindero. 2014. Conditional generative adversarial nets.

Tianrui Niu, Fangxiang Feng, Lingxuan Li, and Xiaojie Wang. 2020. Image synthesis from locally related texts. In *ICMR*.

Augustus Odena, Christopher Olah, and Jonathon Shlens. 2016. Conditional image synthesis with auxiliary classifier gans. In *ICML*.

Scott E. Reed, Zeynep Akata, Xinchen Yan, Lajanugen Logeswaran, Bernt Schiele, and Honglak Lee. 2016. Generative adversarial text to image synthesis. In *ICML*.

Tim Salimans, Ian Goodfellow, Wojciech Zaremba, Vicki Cheung, Alec Radford, and Xi Chen. 2016. Improved techniques for training gans. In *NIPS*.

Mike Schuster and K. Paliwal. 1997. Bidirectional recurrent neural networks. *IEEE Trans. Signal Process.*, 45:2673–2681.

Hao Tan and Mohit Bansal. 2019. Lxmert: Learning cross-modality encoder representations from transformers. *arXiv preprint arXiv:1908.07490*.

Tao Xu, Pengchuan Zhang, Qiuyuan Huang, Han Zhang, Zhe Gan, Xiaolei Huang, and Xiaodong He. 2017. Attngan: Fine-grained text to image generation with attentional generative adversarial networks. In *CVPR*.

Zichao Yang, Xiaodong He, Jianfeng Gao, Li Deng, and Alex Smola. 2016. Stacked attention networks for image question answering. In *CVPR*.

Raymond A. Yeh, Chen Chen, Teck-Yian Lim, Alexander G. Schwing, Mark Hasegawa-Johnson, and Minh N. Do. 2016. Semantic image inpainting with deep generative models. In *CVPR*.

Han Zhang, Tao Xu, and Hongsheng Li. 2016. Stackgan: Text to photo-realistic image synthesis with stacked generative adversarial networks. In *ICCV*.

Han Zhang, Tao Xu, Hongsheng Li, Shaoting Zhang, Xiaogang Wang, Xiaolei Huang, and Dimitris N. Metaxas. 2017. Stackgan++: Realistic image synthesis with stacked generative adversarial networks. *IEEE Transactions on Pattern Analysis and Machine Intelligence*, 41:1947–1962.

Jun-Yan Zhu, Taesung Park, Phillip Isola, and Alexei A. Efros. 2017. Unpaired image-to-image translation using cycle-consistent adversarial networks. In *ICCV*.

Minfeng Zhu, Pingbo Pan, Wei Chen, and Yi Yandg. 2019. Dm-gan: Dynamic memory generative adversarial networks for text-to-image synthesis. In *CVPR*.

Seeing the world through text: Evaluating image descriptions for commonsense reasoning in machine reading comprehension

Diana Galvan-Sosa[1], **Jun Suzuki**[1,2], **Kyosuke Nishida**[3],
Koji Matsuda[2,1], **Kentaro Inui**[1,2]
[1]Tohoku University, [2]RIKEN, [3]NTT Media Intelligence Laboratories
{dianags, jun.suzuki, matsuda}@ecei.tohoku.ac.jp,
kyosuke.nishida.rx@hco.ntt.co.jp,
inui@ecei.tohoku.ac.jp

Abstract

Despite recent achievements in natural language understanding, reasoning over commonsense knowledge still represents a big challenge to AI systems. As the name suggests, common sense is related to perception and as such, humans derive it from experience rather than from literary education. Recent works in the NLP and the computer vision field have made the effort of making such knowledge explicit using written language and visual inputs, respectively. Our premise is that the latter source fits better with the characteristics of commonsense acquisition. In this work, we explore to what extent the descriptions of real-world scenes are sufficient to learn common sense about different daily situations, drawing upon visual information to answer script knowledge questions.

1 Introduction

The recent advances achieved by large neural language models (LMs), such as BERT (Devlin et al., 2018), in natural language understanding tasks like question answering (Rajpurkar et al., 2016) and machine reading comprehension (Lai et al., 2017) are, beyond any doubt, one of the most important accomplishments of modern natural language processing (NLP). These advances suggest that a LM can match a human's stack of knowledge by training on a large text corpora like Wikipedia. Consequently, it has been assumed that through this method, LMs can also acquire some degree of *commonsense* knowledge. It is difficult to find a unique definition, but we can think of *common sense* as something we expect other people to know and regard as obvious (Minsky, 2007). However, when communicating, people tend not to provide information which is obvious or extraneous (as cited in Gordon and Van Durme (2013)). If common sense is something obvious, and therefore less likely to be reported, what LMs can learn from text is already being limited. Liu and Singh (2004) and more recently Rashkin et al. (2018) and Sap et al. (2019) have tried to alleviate this problem by collecting crowdsourced annotations of commonsense knowledge around frequent phrasal events (e.g., PERSONX EATS PASTA FOR DINNER, PERSONX MAKES PERSONY'S COFFEE) extracted from stories and books. From our perspective, the main limitation of this approach is that even if we ask annotators to make explicit information that they will usually omit for being too obvious, the set of commonsense facts about the human world is too large to be listed. Then, what other options are there?

As the name suggests, common sense[1] is related to *perception*, which the Oxford English Dictionary defines as the ability of becoming aware of something through our senses: SIGHT *(e.g., the sky is blue)*, HEARING *(e.g., a dog barks)*, SMELL *(e.g., trash stinks)*, TASTE *(e.g., strawberries are sweet)*, and TOUCH *(e.g., fire is hot)*. Among those, vision (i.e., sight) is one of the primary modalities for humans to learn and reason about the world (Sadeghi et al., 2015). Therefore, we hypothesize that annotations of visual input, like images, are an option to learn about the world without actually experiencing it. This paper explores to what extent the textual descriptions of images about real-world scenes are sufficient to learn common sense about different human daily situations. To this end, we use a large-scale image dataset as knowledge base to improve the performance of a pre-trained LM on a commonsense machine reading comprehension task. We find that by using image descriptions, the model is able to answer some

[1]Latin *sensus* (perception, capability of feeling, ability to percieve)

Proceedings of the Second Workshop on Beyond Vision and LANguage: inTEgrating Real-world kNowledge (LANTERN), pages 23–29
Barcelona, Spain (Online), December 13, 2020

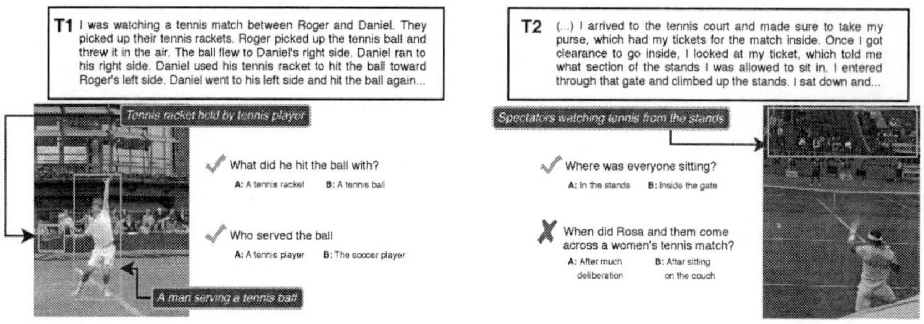

Figure 1: Example of three selected and one removed commonsense questions from two MCScript2.0 instances.

questions about common properties and locations of objects that it previously answered incorrectly. The ultimate goal of our work is to discover an alternative to the expensive (in terms of time) and limited (in terms of coverage) crowdsourced-commonsense acquisition approach.

2 Related work

Knowledge extraction. Previous works have already recognized the rich content of computer vision datasets and investigated its benefits for commonsense knowledge extraction. For instance, Yatskar et al. (2016) and Mukuze et al. (2018) derived 16K commonsense relations and 2,000 verb/location pairs (e.g., *holds*(dining-table, cutlery), *eat*/*restaurant*) from the annotations included in the Microsoft Common Objects in Context dataset (Lin et al., 2014) (MS-COCO). However, they only focused on physical commonsense. A more recent trend is to query LMs for commonsense facts. While a robust LM like BERT has shown a strong performance retrieving commonsense knowledge at a similar level to factual knowledge (Petroni et al., 2019), this seems to happen only when that knowledge is explicitly written down (Forbes et al., 2019).

Machine reading comprehension (MRC). MRC has long been the preferred task to evaluate a machine's understanding of language through questions about a given text. The current most challenging datasets such as Visual Question Answering (Goyal et al., 2017), NarrativeQA (Kočiskỳ et al., 2018), MCScript (Ostermann et al., 2018; Ostermann et al., 2019), CommonsenseQA (Talmor et al., 2018), Visual Commonsense Reasoning (Zellers et al., 2019) and CosmosQA (Huang et al., 2019) were designed to be solvable only by using both context (written or visual) and background knowledge. In all of these datasets, no system has been able to reach the upper bound set by humans. This emphasizes the need to find appropriate sources for systems to equal human knowledge.

Our work lies in the intersection of these two directions. We aim to use computer vision datasets for broad commonsense knowledge acquisition. As a first step, we explore whether visual text from images provides the implicit knowledge needed to answer questions about an MRC text. Ours is an ongoing attempt to emulate the success of multi-modal information in VQA and VCR on a MRC task.

3 Approach

We evaluate image descriptions through a MRC task for which commonsense knowledge is required, and assume that answering a question incorrectly means the reader lacks such knowledge. Most of what humans consider obvious about the world is learned from experience, and we believe there is a fair amount of them written down in an image's description. We will test this idea by using image descriptions as external knowledge. Out of the different types of common sense, the text passages in the selected MRC dataset focus on *script knowledge* (Schank and Abelson, 2013), which covers everyday *scenarios* like BRUSHING TEETH, as well as the *participants* (persons and objects) and the *events* that take place during them. Since scenarios represent activities that we do on a regular basis, we expect to find images of it. Ideally, for each passage, we would automatically query an image dataset to retrieve descriptions related to what the passage is about. Retrieval is a key step in our approach and for the time

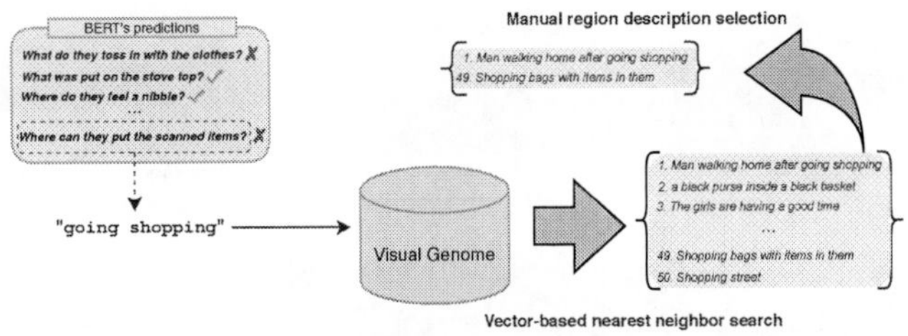

Figure 2: Retrieval process for one of the questions BERT answered incorrectly. Identifying the GOING SHOPPING scenario, querying Visual Genome and selecting the most related region descriptions to the scenario was manually done.

being, such process was done manually so we can focus on the image's description content rather than in the retrieval process itself.

There is a considerable number of crowdsourced image datasets whose image descriptions are available, which means they can be collected (and extended, if needed) for a reasonable cost. The motivation behind our approach is that once such descriptions are proven to contain useful commonsense knowledge that it is not easily obtained from text data, one can think of extending the description collection.

4 Experiments

4.1 Data

Image dataset. Visual Genome (Krishna et al., 2017) is a large-scale collection of non-iconic, real-world images with dense captions for multiple objects and regions in a single image. Each of the 108K images in the dataset has an average of 50 region descriptions of 1 to 16 words. To use this dataset as a knowledge base, we first used BERT-sentence embeddings (Reimers and Gurevych, 2019) to embedded all of the region descriptions and then created a semantic search index using FAISS (Johnson et al., 2017). When querying the index, we retrieved the top 50 results.

Reading comprehension dataset. MCScript2.0 is a dataset with stories about 200 everyday scenarios. Each instance has a text passage paired with a set of questions, which in turn have two answer candidates (one correct and one incorrect). In total, MCScript2.0 has 19,821 questions, out of which 9,935 are commonsense questions that require script knowledge. We split the dataset into train, dev and test sets as in (Ostermann et al., 2019). The train set is used as it is. However, for evaluation, we worked with a subset of 56 and 81 questions from the original dev and test sets, respectively (more details of this in the next section). The subsets include instances with passages about 15 out of the 200 scenarios. For each instance, we took all of its commonsense questions and further selected those in which the necessary commonsense knowledge might be present in one (or more) image descriptions. An example is shown in Figure 1.

4.2 Models

BERT (Baseline). Fine-tuned BERT (base-uncased) on MCScript2.0 using three different random seeds (See Appendix A).

Visually Enhanced BERT. As introduced in Section 3, we hypothesize there is commonsense knowledge present in image descriptions. This model aims to improve on the baseline by using region descriptions from Visual Genome to answer those questions were BERT was wrong. We will refer to these questions as the *unanswerable questions* set. All of them were manually inspected to identify the scenario they are about. As shown in Figure 2, the scenario name is used to query our Visual Genome index. If the results do not contain information about the scenario's events or participants, we refined the query using keywords from the question (e.g., querying "going fishing" returns no results mentioning "rod", a new query would be "going fishing rod"). To be careful not to exceed BERT's sequence length, we selected a maximum of 6 region descriptions from the results and concatenated them at the beginning

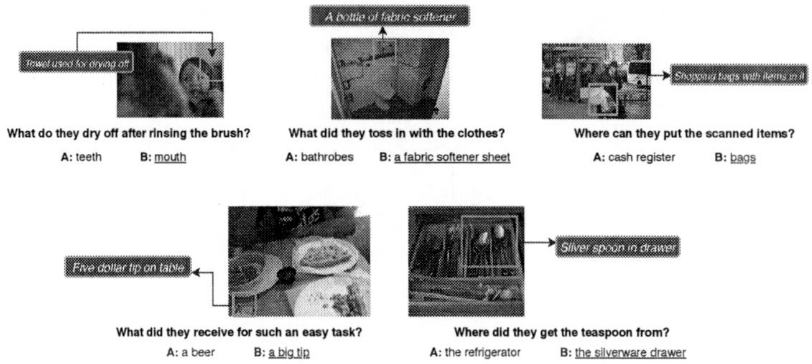

Figure 3: Examples of questions from the unanswerable set and one of the manually selected region descriptions from Visual Genome.

of the given question's text passage. Finally, we fine-tuned the model just as we did with the baseline model.

The whole retrieval process was done manually, which did not represent much of a problem for the dev and test subsets. However, it would be time-consuming to follow this approach with the train set. We fine-tuned on the complete train data, but we limited the use of image descriptions to 225 train questions that were selected in the same way as the dev and test subsets.

5 Results

For most of the questions in the unanswerable set, we did find related region descriptions. Figure 3 shows some of the images retrieved and the regions that matched what the question is asking. Besides its size, one of the main advantages of Visual Genome annotations is that they cover several regions that compose the scene in an image. Thanks to this, we were able to find region descriptions that not only mention an object (e.g., *a towel, scissors, a dollar-bill*), but also add a description of how the object can be used (e.g., *towel used for drying off, scissors for cutting string*) or what does it represent (e.g., *five dollar tip on table*). This suggests that our hypothesis mentioned in Section 1 about annotations of visual input might be correct. As shown in Table 1, region descriptions helped BERT to achieve a better

Model	**Dev** Commonsense	**Test** Commonsense
fine-tuned BERT (base-uncased)	.780	.732
Visually Enhanced BERT	.857	.749

Table 1: Accuracy of BERT baseline and our manually visually enhanced BERT in both MCScript2.0 development and test sets. The results come from three different random seeds.

accuracy. If our hypothesis is true, the improvement should come from correctly answering questions from the unanswerable set. This was true for those related to affordances.[2] Some examples of questions that became answerable for Visually Enhanced BERT are *What did they toss in with the clothes?*, and *What do they cut out the pieces with?*. Another type of question BERT initially had problems answering required commonsense knowledge about an object's location. Some examples of those questions are *Where did they get the teaspoon from?* (Answer: the silverware drawer) and *Where did they get the paper plate from?* (Answer: the kitchen). Our results suggest that region descriptions were more beneficial to these type of questions, since they were no longer unanswerable for Visually Enhanced BERT. However, there were cases in which we could not see an improvement. Questions like *What did they receive for such an easy task?* (Answer: big tip) and *What does a list keep them on?* (Answer: budget) do require commonsense knowledge about the SERVING A DRINK and GOING SHOPPING scenarios, but the

[2]An object's properties that show the possible actions users can make with it.

concept that needs to be understood is too abstract. Even though we found region descriptions that match the correct answer candidate (e.g., *Five dollar tip on table. Tip on the table.*), these type of questions remained unanswerable for Visually Enhanced BERT. See Appendix B for more examples.

In a classic reading comprehension task, word matching usually helps to find the correct answer. However, MCScript2.0 evaluates beyond mere understanding of the text and as such, it was designed to be robust against it. Out of the 56 questions in our dev set, we observed that the number of times a passage mentions the correct and the incorrect answer candidates is similar (42 and 36, respectively) and in either case this seemed to have influenced BERT's predictions. This stayed roughly the same after we appended the region descriptions.

6 Conclusion and Future Work

Pre-trained large LMs have significantly closed the gap between human and computer performance in a wide range of tasks, but the commonsense knowledge they capture is still limited. In this work, we presented a controlled experimental setup to explore the plausibility of acquiring commonsense knowledge from dense image descriptions. Our preliminary results on a commonsense-MRC task suggest that such descriptions contain simple but valuable information that humans naturally build through experiencing the world. In future work, our aim is to automate the retrieval process and explore better ways of using region descriptions than the presented approach of modifying BERT's input format.

Acknowledgements

This work was supported by JST CREST Grant Number JPMJCR1513, Japan. We thank the anonymous reviewers for their insightful comments and suggestions.

References

Jacob Devlin, Ming-Wei Chang, Kenton Lee, and Kristina Toutanova. 2018. Bert: Pre-training of deep bidirectional transformers for language understanding. *arXiv preprint arXiv:1810.04805*.

Maxwell Forbes, Ari Holtzman, and Yejin Choi. 2019. Do neural language representations learn physical commonsense? *arXiv preprint arXiv:1908.02899*.

Jonathan Gordon and Benjamin Van Durme. 2013. Reporting bias and knowledge acquisition. In *Proceedings of the 2013 workshop on Automated knowledge base construction*, pages 25–30.

Yash Goyal, Tejas Khot, Douglas Summers-Stay, Dhruv Batra, and Devi Parikh. 2017. Making the V in VQA matter: Elevating the role of image understanding in Visual Question Answering. In *Conference on Computer Vision and Pattern Recognition (CVPR)*.

Lifu Huang, Ronan Le Bras, Chandra Bhagavatula, and Yejin Choi. 2019. Cosmos qa: Machine reading comprehension with contextual commonsense reasoning. *arXiv preprint arXiv:1909.00277*.

Jeff Johnson, Matthijs Douze, and Hervé Jégou. 2017. Billion-scale similarity search with gpus. *arXiv preprint arXiv:1702.08734*.

Tomáš Kočiský, Jonathan Schwarz, Phil Blunsom, Chris Dyer, Karl Moritz Hermann, Gábor Melis, and Edward Grefenstette. 2018. The narrativeqa reading comprehension challenge. *Transactions of the Association for Computational Linguistics*, 6:317–328.

Ranjay Krishna, Yuke Zhu, Oliver Groth, Justin Johnson, Kenji Hata, Joshua Kravitz, Stephanie Chen, Yannis Kalantidis, Li-Jia Li, David A Shamma, et al. 2017. Visual genome: Connecting language and vision using crowdsourced dense image annotations. *International Journal of Computer Vision*, 123(1):32–73.

Guokun Lai, Qizhe Xie, Hanxiao Liu, Yiming Yang, and Eduard Hovy. 2017. Race: Large-scale reading comprehension dataset from examinations. *arXiv preprint arXiv:1704.04683*.

Tsung-Yi Lin, Michael Maire, Serge Belongie, James Hays, Pietro Perona, Deva Ramanan, Piotr Dollár, and C Lawrence Zitnick. 2014. Microsoft coco: Common objects in context. In *European conference on computer vision*, pages 740–755. Springer.

Hugo Liu and Push Singh. 2004. Conceptnet: a practical commonsense reasoning tool-kit. *BT technology journal*, 22(4):211–226.

Marvin Minsky. 2007. *The emotion machine: Commonsense thinking, artificial intelligence, and the future of the human mind*. Simon and Schuster.

Nelson Mukuze, Anna Rohrbach, Vera Demberg, and Bernt Schiele. 2018. A vision-grounded dataset for predicting typical locations for verbs. In *Proceedings of the Eleventh International Conference on Language Resources and Evaluation (LREC 2018)*.

Simon Ostermann, Ashutosh Modi, Michael Roth, Stefan Thater, and Manfred Pinkal. 2018. Mcscript: A novel dataset for assessing machine comprehension using script knowledge. *arXiv preprint arXiv:1803.05223*.

Simon Ostermann, Michael Roth, and Manfred Pinkal. 2019. Mcscript2. 0: A machine comprehension corpus focused on script events and participants. *arXiv preprint arXiv:1905.09531*.

Fabio Petroni, Tim Rocktäschel, Patrick Lewis, Anton Bakhtin, Yuxiang Wu, Alexander H Miller, and Sebastian Riedel. 2019. Language models as knowledge bases? *arXiv preprint arXiv:1909.01066*.

Pranav Rajpurkar, Jian Zhang, Konstantin Lopyrev, and Percy Liang. 2016. Squad: 100,000+ questions for machine comprehension of text. *arXiv preprint arXiv:1606.05250*.

Hannah Rashkin, Maarten Sap, Emily Allaway, Noah A Smith, and Yejin Choi. 2018. Event2mind: Commonsense inference on events, intents, and reactions. *arXiv preprint arXiv:1805.06939*.

Nils Reimers and Iryna Gurevych. 2019. Sentence-bert: Sentence embeddings using siamese bert-networks. In *Proceedings of the 2019 Conference on Empirical Methods in Natural Language Processing*. Association for Computational Linguistics, 11.

Fereshteh Sadeghi, Santosh K Kumar Divvala, and Ali Farhadi. 2015. Viske: Visual knowledge extraction and question answering by visual verification of relation phrases. In *Proceedings of the IEEE conference on computer vision and pattern recognition*, pages 1456–1464.

Maarten Sap, Ronan Le Bras, Emily Allaway, Chandra Bhagavatula, Nicholas Lourie, Hannah Rashkin, Brendan Roof, Noah A Smith, and Yejin Choi. 2019. Atomic: An atlas of machine commonsense for if-then reasoning. In *Proceedings of the AAAI Conference on Artificial Intelligence*, volume 33, pages 3027–3035.

Roger C Schank and Robert P Abelson. 2013. *Scripts, plans, goals, and understanding: An inquiry into human knowledge structures*. Psychology Press.

Alon Talmor, Jonathan Herzig, Nicholas Lourie, and Jonathan Berant. 2018. Commonsenseqa: A question answering challenge targeting commonsense knowledge. *arXiv preprint arXiv:1811.00937*.

Mark Yatskar, Vicente Ordonez, and Ali Farhadi. 2016. Stating the obvious: Extracting visual common sense knowledge. In *Proceedings of the 2016 Conference of the North American Chapter of the Association for Computational Linguistics: Human Language Technologies*, pages 193–198.

Rowan Zellers, Yonatan Bisk, Ali Farhadi, and Yejin Choi. 2019. From recognition to cognition: Visual commonsense reasoning. In *Proceedings of the IEEE Conference on Computer Vision and Pattern Recognition*, pages 6720–6731.

A Appendix A. Implementation

A.1 Input format

We fine-tuned a vanilla-BERT with the following input configuration: the question and one of its answer candidates are appended to segment one and the text passage is appended to segment two. Therefore, we have two inputs per instance. To help BERT differentiate between the question and answer-candidate tokens, we used a special separator token[3]. The maximum sequence length was set to 384. We trained the model up to 5 epochs with a learning rate (Adam) of 5e-5 and a training batch size of 8 using 3 different random seeds.

B Appendix B. Input and output examples

Figure 4 shows how we build the input representation of two MCScript2.0 questions. The question and answer candidate A in segment one, and the text passage in segment two. Similarly, there is a second input representation with the question and answer candidate B in segment one, and the text passage in segment two. BERT computes a softmax over the two choices to predict the correct answer candidate. Visually Enhanced BERT builds the input in a similar way. The difference is that the manually selected region descriptions are appended at the beginning of the text passage. The number of tokens in the text passage increases, but the input configuration remains the same.

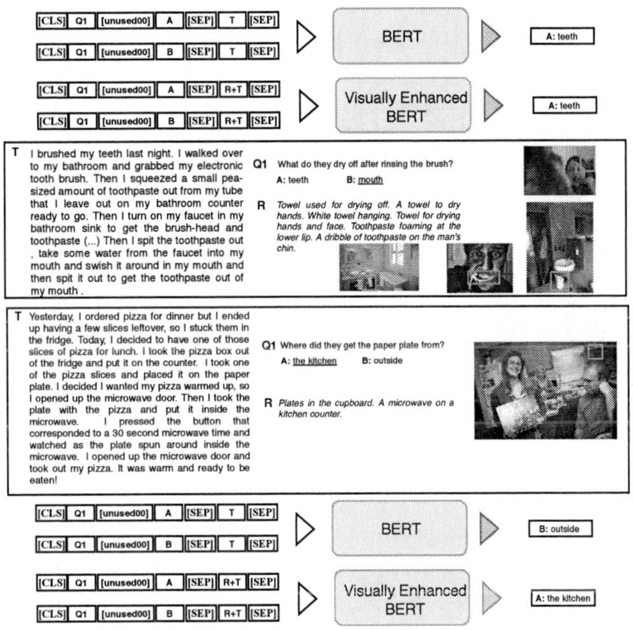

Figure 4: Two input/output examples. In the top example, region descriptions were not helpful to chose the correct answer candidate. In the bottom example, they were.

[3]We used '[unused00]' as the special separator token, which is included in BERT's vocabulary

How do image description systems describe people? A targeted assessment of system competence in the PEOPLE domain

Emiel van Miltenburg
Tilburg center for Cognition and Communication
Tilburg University
Warandelaan 2, 5037 AB Tilburg, The Netherlands
C.W.J.vanMiltenburg@tilburguniversity.edu

Abstract

Evaluations of image description systems are typically domain-general: generated descriptions for the held-out test images are either compared to a set of reference descriptions (using automated metrics), or rated by human judges on one or more Likert scales (for fluency, overall quality, and other quality criteria). While useful, these evaluations do not tell us anything about the kinds of image descriptions that systems are able to produce. Or, phrased differently, these evaluations do not tell us anything about the cognitive capabilities of image description systems. This paper proposes a different kind of assessment, that is able to quantify the extent to which these systems are able to describe humans. This assessment is based on a manual characterization (a context-free grammar) of English entity labels in the PEOPLE domain, to determine the range of possible outputs. We examined 9 systems to see what kinds of labels they actually use. We found that these systems only use a small subset of at most 13 different kinds of modifiers (e.g. *tall* and *short* modify HEIGHT, *sad* and *happy* modify MOOD), but 27 kinds of modifiers are never used. Future research could study these semantic dimensions in more detail.

1 Introduction

Image description systems are typically trained and evaluated using datasets of described images, such as Flickr30K and MS COCO (Young et al., 2014; Lin et al., 2014). Automated metrics such as BLEU, Meteor, and CIDEr compare the generated descriptions to a set of reference descriptions, and produce a textual similarity score (Papineni et al., 2002; Denkowski and Lavie, 2014; Vedantam et al., 2015). The overall score is said to convey the performance of the system. These metrics (and especially BLEU) are often criticized because of their low correlation to human ratings (Elliott and Keller, 2014; Kilickaya et al., 2017; Reiter, 2018). Human ratings, in turn, are typically collected using Likert scales, where participants rate descriptions for their fluency, correctness, overall quality, and other quality criteria (van der Lee et al., 2019). While these measures do afford us with some insight into system performance, they are very general, and not tied to any specific cognitive ability (e.g. to produce descriptions containing negations, to reason about past and future events, or to successfully refer to properties or entities in a particular domain). This is a problem because it means we do not know what systems are good or bad at.[1] Perhaps the most informative metric in common use is SPICE (Anderson et al., 2016), which enables researchers to assess the ability of image description systems to produce color terms, for example, by computing precision/recall of these terms with regard to a scene graph representing the relevant image.

Instead of general evaluation metrics, we propose to develop specific metrics to assess[2] whether image description systems are able to produce specific kinds of descriptions. This paper presents a proof-of-concept to assess the extent to which systems are able to produce different kinds of person-labels. Our main idea is that, to assess model performance, we should first characterize the domain of interest, such that we have a clear sense of the range of possible descriptions. Following this characterisation, we can

[1]For a more in-depth discussion of this point, see (Schlangen, 2019; Schlangen, 2020).

[2]Throughout this paper, we deliberately use the term *assessment* instead of *evaluation*, to emphasise that we are interested in characterising model behaviour, rather than determining whether this behaviour is good or bad.

Proceedings of the Second Workshop on Beyond Vision and LANguage: inTEgrating Real-world kNowledge (LANTERN), pages 30–36
Barcelona, Spain (Online), December 13, 2020

see whether the model outputs cover the full range (which is unlikely), or whether it produces a small subset of the possible descriptions. Our starting point is the taxonomy of person-labels developed by van Miltenburg et al. (2018b), who manually categorised all person-labels in the Flickr30K (Young et al., 2014) and Visual Genome (Krishna et al., 2017) datasets (both US English), with the head nouns *male, female, males, females, man, woman, men, women, boy, girl, boys* and *girls*. They implemented their categorisation scheme in a context-free grammar (CFG; using NLTK (Loper and Bird, 2002)), so that all combinations of modifiers and head nouns would be covered. To illustrate: with only two modifiers (*tall* and *happy*) and 12 head nouns, there are already 48 possible combinations (24 with single modifiers, and another 24 with both modifiers in two different orders). All variations can be captured by the following CFG rules (where commas are used to indicate a choice between different terminals):

LABEL → DET MOD NOUN
MOD → MOD MOD
MOD → MOOD
MOD → HEIGHT
DET → *the, a*
NOUN → *man, woman, ...*
MOOD → *happy, sad, angry*
HEIGHT → *tall, short*

The original CFG is limited to the eight head nouns specified above. We extended the grammar to obtain broader coverage of system output data (both in terms of head nouns and in terms of modifiers). We then used the grammar to analyse this data, and to see what kinds of labels are typically produced by image description systems. We found that systems are limited in their coverage: at most 13 out of 40 modifier categories were used. This means that 26 different kinds of semantic properties that are attested in human image description data, cannot be found in the output data.[3]

2 Method

Corpus data. van Miltenburg et al. (2018b) developed two taxonomies using English corpus data from Flickr30K and the Visual Genome dataset (the latter dataset contains 108,077 images from MS COCO). For this paper, we merged the two taxonomies to have broader coverage. After combining the different sets of words for each category, we manually inspected and revised the category files.[4]

System data. We use output data from nine different image description systems, collected by van Miltenburg et al. (2018a), who obtained this data by contacting the authors of all image description papers that appeared in conferences and journals in 2016-2017. All systems were trained o the MS COCO training set, and all descriptions were generated for the MS COCO validation set (40,504 images). Although the systems are slightly older, many are still competitive with the state-of-the-art. Furthermore, we do not want to make any claims about current model performance. Rather, our aim is to provide a proof-of-concept of a new assessment procedure for image description systems.

Preparation. We updated the grammar in two stages. In the first stage, we added more head nouns. People are not just referred to using gendered nouns. Some are referred to using their occupation (*police officer*) or their (social) role (*friend, neighbour, mother*). Thus we added more categories (with corresponding lexical items) for different kinds of head nouns. This required us to determine which nouns refer to people. Because this experiment is a proof-of-concept, we focus only on the nouns that actually occur in the output data for the systems mentioned above. We used SpaCy (Honnibal and Montani, 2017) to identify noun chunks in the generated descriptions, and identified 5385 unique sequences of one or more nouns (assuming that multiple nouns together form compound nouns). We then manually selected 170 heads that refer to people and developed category labels for all different kinds of nouns, adding new labels until all nouns were categorised. A single head may be part of multiple different categories, and thus receive multiple labels. Some examples are provided in Table 1.

In the second stage, we updated the set of modifiers. Since different head nouns may be modified in different ways, we extended coverage of the modifiers to include the ones that are used for nouns other than the twelve original nouns. This was done by identifying all noun chunks that refer to people (i.e. end with one of the heads identified in the previous step), analysing them with our updated grammar, and manually categorising all modifiers that weren't already covered by our grammar. We found that the

[3]All code and data is available at: `https://github.com/evanmiltenburg/AnalysePeopleDescriptions`.
[4]Details about this procedure (with data at each step of the process) are in the GitHub repository.

ACTIVITY	baseball player, commuter, kite surfer, pedestrian, runner, skier, swimmer, spectators
AGE	adult, baby, babies, child, children, kid, toddler, girl, lady, woman, women, man, men
GENDERED	boy, girl, man, females, woman, ladies, bride, groom, daughter, cowboy, camera man
PLURAL OR MASS NOUNS	crowd, passengers, persons, business people, construction workers, students, spectators
RELATION	father, friend, patient, bride, daughter, couple, family, friends, owner, customer, spectators
STATUS OR OCCUPATION	clown, coach, police officer, farmer, king, camera man, students, emergency personnel

Table 1: Different noun categories used in our grammar, with examples for each category.

System	#Labels	#Mods	Avg-mods	Mod-cats	Noun-cats
Tavakoli et al. (2017)	14039	1676	0.12	4	6
Zhou et al. (2017)	14698	1792	0.12	4	6
Vinyals et al. (2017)	15496	1165	0.08	5	6
Shetty et al. (2016)	15247	1514	0.1	4	6
Dai et al. (2017)	14793	1763	0.12	13	6
Mun et al. (2017)	15645	1906	0.12	3	6
Shetty et al. (2017)	14558	1861	0.13	10	6
Liu et al. (2017)	13856	1296	0.09	3	6
Wu et al. (2017)	14486	2060	0.14	5	6

Table 2: Overall statistics for the nine different systems. Columns show the total number of labels referring to humans, the total number of modifiers used, the average number of modifiers per label, the number of modifier categories, and the number of noun categories.

system outputs contain 667 unique noun chunks that refer to people. Of these, 562 (84%) were already covered by the grammar with the new heads included. This meant we had to check 105 noun chunks (16%) for additional modifiers to include in the grammar. We updated the grammar until there were 5 ungrammatical phrases (0.75%) left that were impossible to categorise.[5] During this process, we added three more nominal heads that were initially overlooked ('traffic girl', 'toy boy' and 'mounted police officers'). The largest gains in coverage were not achieved by adding more modifiers, but by adding the UNK token (occurring in 11 chunks), determiners (*their, these, this*, 16 cases), and quantifiers (*some, many, several*, 38 cases).

Analysis. We analysed the data from all nine systems, using our context-free grammar, to see which modifier and head noun categories are most frequent. Figure 1 shows an example analysis, resulting in the modifier categories HEIGHT and MOOD, and the noun category AGENOUN. We assume that each modifier category is used only once per noun chunk. Some labels are ambiguous, resulting in multiple possible analyses. In those cases, we take the union of all possible labels. This does overestimate model performance, so any deeper analysis of system output should inspect the results to find example usages for each category.

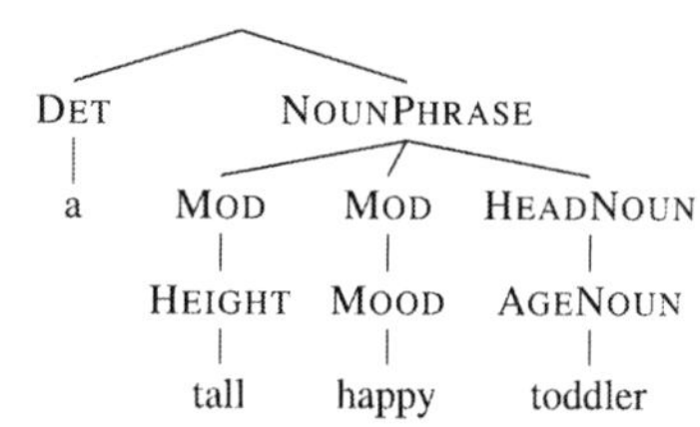

Figure 1: Parse tree for the label: *a tall happy toddler.*

3 Results

Table 2 shows the overall statistics for our corpus of system outputs. We find that the systems differ in the amount of person-labels that they generate. The system from Mun et al. generates 1,789 more person-labels than the system from Liu et al. The system from Vinyals et al. produces the lowest average number of modifiers per person-label. Overall, the systems only use a subset of potential modifier categories: only four to thirteen different kinds of modifiers, while there are 40 different categories in our grammar.

What categories are produced? When we look at the nouns and modifiers that are produced by all systems, we find that all systems produce the same noun types. The story is different for the modifiers, where we find the totals given in Table 3. So, for example, only Dai et al.'s system produced one or more descriptions referring to someone's height: *a short young boy* (analysed as: HEIGHT, AGE,

[5]These were: *a near a crowd, a womans lady, cars police, lawn women, two cut men*

Category	Examples	Total	Systems
AGE	a *baby* boy, a *middle aged* surfer, a pretty *young* man, an *old* lady	9	All
BUILD	a *tiny* baby, a *small* adult/baby/boy/child/girl/kid, a *big* cute little girl	9	All
OCCUPATIONSOCGROUP	the *professional* player/skier, a *little league baseball* player	9	All
ACTIVITY	a *large commercial airplane flying* commuter, a *newly married* couple	6	1,3,4,5,7,9
MOOD	a *happy* boy/child, a *smiling* boy/child/lady/man/woman/young lady	3	5,7,9
ATTRACTIVENESS	a *beautiful* woman/young lady/blond woman, a *cute* baby	3	3,5,7
HAIRCOLOR	a beautiful *blond* woman, a beautiful *blonde* lady, a *blonde* woman	2	5,7
SKINCOLOR	a *dark* woman, a *white* baby, a *white* tennis player, a *yellow* lifeguard	2	5,7
AMOUNTOFCLOTHING	a *naked* baby/child/girl/lady/man/woman, a *shirtless* child/man	2	2,7
NUMBER	a *couple* kids/women, a *few* employees/kids, a *lone* skier/surfer	2	5,7
HEIGHT	a *short* young boy, a *tall* man, the *short* men	1	5
ETHNICITY	an *asian* boy/woman	1	5
JUDGMENT	an *old fashioned man*	1	5
KINDOFCLOTHING	a *hat* adult	1	5

Systems legend: 1: Tavakoli et al. (2017), 2: Zhou et al. (2017), 3: Vinyals et al. (2017), 4: Shetty et al. (2016)
5: Dai et al. (2017), 6: Mun et al. (2017), 7: Shetty et al. (2017), 8: Liu et al. (2017), 9: Wu et al. (2017)

Table 3: Different modifier categories, with examples from the machine-generated output. Modifiers are marked in *italics*. Similar phrases using the same modifier with different nouns are indicated using forward slashes. The last two columns refer to the number of systems producing descriptions containing the relevant types of modifiers.

GENDEREDNOUN/AGENOUN). This might be due to their GAN-based approach, which aims to make descriptions more human-like.

Some observations. Below are some initial observations about the results:

Lack of diversity. The descriptions are not very diverse (van Miltenburg et al., 2018a), and this is reflected in our data: there is little variation within each of the categories. For example, in the BUILD category, only three adjectives (out of 48 possible modifiers) are used: *big, small* and *tiny*.

Overgeneralisation. Our parser overgeneralises. For example, when we take a closer look at the labels containing modifiers relating to the BUILD of a person (e.g., *big, small, tiny*), we find multiple instances where these modifiers are not used in the relevant sense, namely: *a big crowd, a small family, a small team*. This shows that manual analysis is currently still necessary (and the system would clearly benefit from word sense disambiguation), but our parser serves as a good filter: without it, it would not be possible to find different kinds of modifiers at all. With the parser and some manual effort, we have a better picture of the kinds of person-labels a system is able to produce.

Biases. The generated labels seem to be biased with respect to gender and ethnicity (cf. van Miltenburg (2016)). For example: ATTRACTIVENESS modifiers are used almost exclusively with women and children. The only counter-example is ambiguous: 'a *pretty* young man' (pretty young or pretty man). HAIRCOLOR is only specified for women. ETHNICITY is only marked for Asian people.

4 Discussion

(Un)intended use of this work. We intended this work to be used in two ways:

1. As a means to assess the extent to which image description systems are able to produce person-descriptions. This is useful because it allows further investigation of the output: we can use our results to see whether these descriptions are warranted by the images (cf. van Miltenburg (2016)), or investigate whether different kinds of person-labels are fairly distributed across different social groups (cf. Otterbacher et al. (2019)).
2. As a more general example of a targeted assessment procedure. The main takeaway from this paper is that it is possible to assess the ability of image description systems to produce different kinds of PEOPLE-descriptions (and this approach could probably be generalised to other domains).

The generation of person-descriptions is a sensitive area of research, which should be treated with care (Todorov et al., 2013; Agüera y Arcas et al., 2017). Not all of the possible labels in our CFG should be generated by image description systems, because they may be offensive when misapplied, offensive in general, or simply impossible to predict on the basis of visual features alone. Our work is expressly *not* intended to encourage the production of ever more detailed person-descriptions, since there are clear dual use issues in this area of research.[6,7]

Competence, performance and accuracy. So far we have treated system competence as 'generating descriptions with particular features.' This is a simplification on two counts:

1. It conflates competence and performance (Chomsky, 1965). Systems that don't generate descriptions with particular features for a given set of images, may still be able to generate such descriptions for other images. (Although one might wonder, with the size of the MS COCO validation set, whether those systems would *ever* generate descriptions with the relevant features.)
2. It ignores the accuracy of the generated person-labels, which is essential for being a competent language-user. A full assessment of system competence should include a human evaluation of the different kinds of labels. For example, judges could rate the accuracy of a stratified sample of machine-generated labels from each of the different categories.

Limitations. This work is a proof-of-concept, and our results should be evaluated as such. We have shown that it is possible to characterise an output domain using a context-free grammar, and that we can use such a grammar to assess what kinds of labels are produced by an image description system. Any statistics should be treated as preliminary.

Annotations. Although we took care to double-check all the labels, the taxonomy has been developed by a single annotator. Future work should investigate the replicability of our taxonomy. (Although there are as many taxonomies as taxonomists, and some amount of disagreement is inevitable, there should be a clear overlap between our data and future replications.)

Coverage. Our taxonomy is driven by existing sets of descriptions. Should image description systems become more creative in the future, or rely on different datasets, then this will affect the coverage of our taxonomy, and updates will be necessary. We do believe that this process could be automated, and that it is feasible to update the taxonomy in a matter of days (which we believe is acceptable, and proportionate to the development time of a new image description system).

Ambiguity. As mentioned in the results section, a context-free grammar is not powerful enough to disambiguate different word senses. So although our parser can act as a filter to select relevant noun phrases from system outputs, this will result in false positives for different modifiers. To reduce this issue, one could either refine our taxonomy and tie it to the output of word sense disambiguation systems, or manually correct the outputs of our parser to create a training set, turning description categorisation into a sequence labeling problem. The latter solution would hopefully also generalise to unseen nouns and modifiers, reducing coverage issues caused by our grounded-in-data approach.

5 Conclusion

Our work shows that it is feasible to assess how image description systems label people, using a context-free grammar. This idea could be applied more broadly, to assess systems' coverage of the original training data (i.e. which patterns the system managed to capture). The development of a taxonomy of expressions in a particular domain does represent a serious time investment, but once this is done, we can more closely assess system performance in a particular domain, for any number of systems. (And perhaps this is also just the cost of wanting to develop end-to-end systems using crowdsourced image description corpora.) As noted by van Miltenburg et al. (2018b), developing a taxonomy also forces us to think about the desirability of different kinds of expressions that may be used in the generated descriptions. This will hopefully lead to improved image description guidelines, which may later be formalised in an assessment procedure, similar to the one reported in this paper.

[6]Dual use refers to the idea that technology can be used both for good and for nefarious purposes (Hovy and Spruit, 2016).

[7]On a related note, visually impaired technology advocate Chancey Fleet has said that she "[worries] that the beneficence that kind of surrounds accessibility technology, this idea we have that accessibility is always a universal good, has created a situation where blind people and our perceived needs can be used to normalize facial recognition in private and semiprivate spaces" (Morris et al., 2020). Whenever researchers believe computer vision technology may help visually impaired users, it is necessary to confirm with these people whether they would indeed appreciate this technology, and whether they believe it is worth any potential negative implications, such as increased surveillance and a further invasion of privacy.

References

Blaise Agüera y Arcas, Margaret Mitchell, and Alexander Todorov. 2017. Physiognomy's new clothes. Medium, May 17.

Peter Anderson, Basura Fernando, Mark Johnson, and Stephen Gould. 2016. Spice: Semantic propositional image caption evaluation. In Bastian Leibe, Jiri Matas, Nicu Sebe, and Max Welling, editors, *Computer Vision – ECCV 2016*, pages 382–398, Cham. Springer International Publishing.

Noam Chomsky. 1965. *Aspects of the Theory of Syntax*. MIT Press.

Bo Dai, Sanja Fidler, Raquel Urtasun, and Dahua Lin. 2017. Towards diverse and natural image descriptions via a conditional gan. In *Proceedings of the 2017 International Conference on Computer Vision*, pages 2970–2979, Venice, Italy.

Michael Denkowski and Alon Lavie. 2014. Meteor universal: Language specific translation evaluation for any target language. In *Proceedings of the Ninth Workshop on Statistical Machine Translation*, pages 376–380, Baltimore, Maryland, USA, June. Association for Computational Linguistics.

Desmond Elliott and Frank Keller. 2014. Comparing automatic evaluation measures for image description. In *Proceedings of the 52nd Annual Meeting of the Association for Computational Linguistics (Volume 2: Short Papers)*, pages 452–457, Baltimore, Maryland, June. Association for Computational Linguistics.

Matthew Honnibal and Ines Montani. 2017. spaCy 2: Natural language understanding with Bloom embeddings, convolutional neural networks and incremental parsing. To appear. See `https://spacy.io` or `https://github.com/explosion/spaCy`.

Dirk Hovy and Shannon L. Spruit. 2016. The social impact of natural language processing. In *Proceedings of the 54th Annual Meeting of the Association for Computational Linguistics (Volume 2: Short Papers)*, pages 591–598, Berlin, Germany, August. Association for Computational Linguistics.

Mert Kilickaya, Aykut Erdem, Nazli Ikizler-Cinbis, and Erkut Erdem. 2017. Re-evaluating automatic metrics for image captioning. In *Proceedings of the 15th Conference of the European Chapter of the Association for Computational Linguistics: Volume 1, Long Papers*, pages 199–209, Valencia, Spain, April. Association for Computational Linguistics.

Ranjay Krishna, Yuke Zhu, Oliver Groth, Justin Johnson, Kenji Hata, Joshua Kravitz, Stephanie Chen, Yannis Kalantidis, Li-Jia Li, David A. Shamma, Michael S. Bernstein, and Li Fei-Fei. 2017. Visual genome: Connecting language and vision using crowdsourced dense image annotations. *International Journal of Computer Vision*, 123(1):32–73.

Tsung-Yi Lin, Michael Maire, Serge Belongie, James Hays, Pietro Perona, Deva Ramanan, Piotr Dollár, and C. Lawrence Zitnick. 2014. Microsoft coco: Common objects in context. In David Fleet, Tomas Pajdla, Bernt Schiele, and Tinne Tuytelaars, editors, *Computer Vision – ECCV 2014*, pages 740–755, Cham. Springer International Publishing.

Chang Liu, Fuchun Sun, Changhu Wang, Feng Wang, and Alan Yuille. 2017. Mat: A multimodal attentive translator for image captioning. In *IJCAI*, pages 4033–4039.

Edward Loper and Steven Bird. 2002. Nltk: The natural language toolkit. In *Proceedings of the ACL-02 Workshop on Effective tools and methodologies for teaching natural language processing and computational linguistics-Volume 1*, pages 63–70. Association for Computational Linguistics.

Meredith Ringel Morris, Cynthia Bennett, Chancey Fleet, and Venkatesh Potluri. 2020. Vizwiz grand challenge workshop at cvpr 2020 - panel discussion with blind technology experts. Video available through YouTube: `https://www.youtube.com/watch?v=f613diLbVAc`, workshop address: `https://vizwiz.org/workshops/2020-workshop/`.

Jonghwan Mun, Minsu Cho, and Bohyung Han. 2017. Text-guided attention model for image captioning. In *AAAI Conference on Artificial Intelligence*.

Jahna Otterbacher, Pınar Barlas, Styliani Kleanthous, and Kyriakos Kyriakou. 2019. How do we talk about other people? group (un)fairness in natural language image descriptions. In *Proceedings of the Seventh AAAI Conference on Human Computation and Crowdsourcing*, pages 106–114. Association for the Advancement of Artificial Intelligence (AAAI).

Kishore Papineni, Salim Roukos, Todd Ward, and Wei-Jing Zhu. 2002. Bleu: a method for automatic evaluation of machine translation. In *Proceedings of the 40th Annual Meeting of the Association for Computational Linguistics*, pages 311–318, Philadelphia, Pennsylvania, USA, July. Association for Computational Linguistics.

Ehud Reiter. 2018. A structured review of the validity of BLEU. *Computational Linguistics*, 44(3):393–401, September.

David Schlangen. 2019. Language tasks and language games: On methodology in current natural language processing research. *CoRR*, abs/1908.10747.

David Schlangen. 2020. Targeting the benchmark: On methodology in current natural language processing research. *CoRR*, abs/2007.04792.

Rakshith Shetty, Hamed R.-Tavakoli, and Jorma Laaksonen. 2016. Exploiting scene context for image captioning. In *Proceedings of the 2016 ACM Workshop on Vision and Language Integration Meets Multimedia Fusion*, iV&L-MM '16, pages 1–8, New York, NY, USA. ACM.

Rakshith Shetty, Marcus Rohrbach, Lisa Anne Hendricks, Mario Fritz, and Bernt Schiele. 2017. Speaking the same language: Matching machine to human captions by adversarial training. In *ICCV*, Oct.

Hamed R Tavakoli, Rakshith Shetty, Ali Borji, and Jorma Laaksonen. 2017. Paying attention to descriptions generated by image captioning models. In *CVPR*, pages 2487–2496.

Alexander Todorov, Peter Mende-Siedlecki, and Ron Dotsch. 2013. Social judgments from faces. *Current opinion in neurobiology*, 23(3):373–380.

Chris van der Lee, Albert Gatt, Emiel van Miltenburg, Sander Wubben, and Emiel Krahmer. 2019. Best practices for the human evaluation of automatically generated text. In *Proceedings of the 12th International Conference on Natural Language Generation*, pages 355–368, Tokyo, Japan, October–November. Association for Computational Linguistics.

Emiel van Miltenburg, Desmond Elliott, and Piek Vossen. 2018a. Measuring the diversity of automatic image descriptions. In *Proceedings of the 27th International Conference on Computational Linguistics*, pages 1730–1741, Santa Fe, New Mexico, USA, August. Association for Computational Linguistics.

Emiel van Miltenburg, Desmond Elliott, and Piek Vossen. 2018b. Talking about other people: an endless range of possibilities. In *Proceedings of the 11th International Conference on Natural Language Generation*, pages 415–420, Tilburg University, The Netherlands, November. Association for Computational Linguistics.

Emiel van Miltenburg. 2016. Stereotyping and bias in the flickr30k dataset. In Jens Edlund, Dirk Heylen, and Patrizia Paggio, editors, *Proceedings of Multimodal Corpora: Computer vision and language processing (MMC 2016)*, pages 1–4.

R. Vedantam, C. L. Zitnick, and D. Parikh. 2015. Cider: Consensus-based image description evaluation. In *2015 IEEE Conference on Computer Vision and Pattern Recognition (CVPR)*, pages 4566–4575.

Oriol Vinyals, Alexander Toshev, Samy Bengio, and Dumitru Erhan. 2017. Show and tell: Lessons learned from the 2015 mscoco image captioning challenge. *IEEE Transactions on Pattern Analysis and Machine Intelligence*, 39(4):652–663, April.

Qi Wu, Chunhua Shen, Peng Wang, Anthony Dick, and Anton van den Hengel. 2017. Image captioning and visual question answering based on attributes and external knowledge. *IEEE Transactions on Pattern Analysis and Machine Intelligence*.

Peter Young, Alice Lai, Micah Hodosh, and Julia Hockenmaier. 2014. From image descriptions to visual denotations: New similarity metrics for semantic inference over event descriptions. *Transactions of the Association for Computational Linguistics*, 2:67–78.

Luowei Zhou, Chenliang Xu, Parker Koch, and Jason J Corso. 2017. Watch what you just said: Image captioning with text-conditional attention. In *Proceedings of the ACM International Conference on Multimedia Thematic Workshops*.

Association for Computational Linguistics
209 N. Eighth Street
Stroudsburg, Pennsylvania 18360

ISBN 978-1-7138-2829-7

CURRAN ASSOCIATES INC.
proceedings.com